Barrett-Jackson®

THE WORLD'S GREATEST COLLECTOR CAR EVENT™

LARRY EDSALL

MOTORBOOKS

DEDICATION

For Nellie Jackson, the matriarch of the company.

ACKNOWLEDGMENTS

The author gratefully acknowledges interviews with Craig Jackson, Nellie Jackson, and Steve Davis of the Barrett-Jackson Auction Company, as well as the considerable help of Gary Bennett and Shelly Drake. In addition, particular note must be made of the help from Ginger Wilber, Barrett-Jackson photograph manager, and from Jamie Breitbach, Barrett-Jackson project manager. Without their long hours and dedicated efforts this book could not have been produced. In addition, marketing manager Deb Klien-Stokes put many hours into this project. Also offering assistance were Patrick van den Bossche and Mike Laurel of Barrett-Jackson, Judi Yates of Schneider-Yates & Associates, and Bob Golfen of the *Arizona Republic*, who shared their insights into the auction and collector car lifestyle.

First published in 2006 by Motorbooks, an imprint of MBI Publishing Company, Galtier Plaza, Suite 200, 380 Jackson Street, St. Paul, MN 55101-3885 USA

MBI Publishing Company titles are also available at discounts in bulk quantity for industrial or sales-promotional use. For details write to Special Sales Manager at MBI Publishing Company, Galtier Plaza, Suite 200, 380 Jackson Street, St. Paul, MN 55101-3885 USA

ISBN-13: 978-0-7603-2779-1
ISBN-10: 0-7603-2779-3

Editor: Jennifer Johnson
Designer: Sara Grindle

Printed in China

Unless specified, all photography by Barrett-Jackson Auction Company, Craig Jackson, Brian Jackson, Steve Davis, Keith Alstrin, Ginger Wilber, Tony Riddick. Don Williams, and Jason Rose.

On the front cover: Nationally televised coverage of the bidding battle for the Oldsmobile F-88 concept car, created by Harley Earl and his design staff at General Motors for the 1954 Motorama tour, rocketed the Barrett-Jackson Auction into the consciousness of auto enthusiasts across the country in 2005.

On the endpapers: Catalog covers by: 1989 Unknown; 1990 Tom Hale; 1991 Al Wilson; 1992 Tom Hale; 1993 Eric Herrrmann; 1994 Tom Hale; 1995 Tom Hale; 1996 Tom Hale; 1997 Tom Hale; 1998 Tom Hale; 1999 George Angelini; 2000 Harold Cleworth; 2001 Harold Cleworth; 2002 Alain Levesque; 2003 Alain Levesque; 2004 Barry Rowe; 2005 Dennis Brown; 2006 Dennis Brown

On the frontispiece: Craig Jackson's enthusiasm for what the Barrett-Jackson event has become is obvious.

On the title page and middle back cover: The Pontiac Bonneville Special was a concept car created by General Motors for its 1954 Motorama tour. The car was designed to launch Pontiac as GM's performance division and took its name from the Bonneville Salt Flats, where world land speed records were set.

On the back cover: (Top) The Parade of Progress was a national tour staged by General Motors as a sneak peek of the way science and technology promised to improve the lives of all Americans. The tour traveled in specially created buses, called Futurliners. One of those customized stages on wheels sold for an astounding $4.32 million at Barrett-Jackson in 2006. (Bottom) At the microphone is Craig Jackson, who took over the family collector car auction business after his father, Russ, and Craig's older brother, Brian, died less than two years apart. Under Craig Jackson's leadership, the Barrett-Jackson Auction has grown into a nationally televised event and a lifestyle event that reaches well beyond the collector car hobby.

Table of contents: (Top) This 1954 Pontiac Bonneville Special Motorama concept car was created after GM design chief Harley Earl returned from watching speed runs on the Bonneville Salt Flats. It sold at Barrett-Jackson in 2006 for $3,024,000. (Second) This 1952 Chrysler d'Elegance sold for $1.188 million at Barrett-Jackson in 2006. (Third) This 1970 HEMI 'Cuda is one of only 14 built, and sold for $2.160 million at the 2006 Barrett-Jackson auction. (Bottom) Craig Jackson has turned an auction into a lifestyle. His passion for the Barrett-Jackson Collector Car Event shows in all he does.

Library of Congress Cataloging-in-Publication Data

Edsall, Larry.
  Barrett-Jackson : the world's greatest collector car event / Larry Edsall.
    p. cm.
    ISBN-13: 978-0-7603-2779-1 (hardbound w/ jacket)
    ISBN-10: 0-7603-2779-3 (hardbound w/ jacket)
1. Barrett-Jackson. 2. Automobile auctions--Arizona--Scottsdale. 3. Automobile auctions--Florida--Palm Beach. 4. Antique and classic cars--Collectors and collecting--United States. I. Title.
TL7.U62S38 2006
629.222075--dc22
                                    2006019493

CONTENTS

FOREWORD

A frequent Barrett-Jackson participant and custom car collector is Bill Goldberg, of World Wrestling fame.

I've loved fast cars for as long as I can remember. My obsession, especially for 1960s and 1970s American muscle cars, has been a major driving force in my life. Through hard work and a bit of luck, I've fed my hunger to collect some truly wonderful cars. More important, I've been able to share this passion with other "automanics" whose fanaticism equals mine.

The Barrett-Jackson Auction has been a big part of my automotive lifestyle. I can clearly remember my first time at the Scottsdale, Arizona, event. The spectacular cars, wild action, TV cameras, and outrageous personalities were intoxicating. Like anyone else who has stepped into this ring, I was immediately hooked.

Having been both a bidder and seller, I've learned a great deal about the team at Barrett-Jackson. These people are not bean counters selling cars this week and art the next. Everyone from the Jackson family and Steve Davis to the guy taking tickets at the door is passionate about car collecting. You just can't fake that kind of enthusiasm. They're as crazy about the hobby as I am, which makes for a truly compelling experience.

Every year, Barrett-Jackson gathers the world's greatest cars in one spot. Looking for a Corvette? There are a hundred available, covering every year of production. Do you want a vintage Ferrari, Shelby GT500, classic Packard, Chip Foose custom, or a HEMI 'Cuda? Take your pick, because it will be at Barrett-Jackson.

It's impossible to overstate the important innovations Barrett-Jackson has pioneered that allow anyone to join the action. From broadcasting the events live on TV to introducing Internet bidding, there's no reason to watch from the sidelines.

The level playing field is especially appealing to me. Everyone from billionaires to the newest hobbyist is treated as a VIP. The rules to participate are the same for everyone in what may be the most competitive environment in the world because the market sets all values. And as someone who lives to compete, the chance to snag the best deal or earn top dollar for one of my cars is addictive.

I once bought three spectacular muscle cars during the Scottsdale auction while I was overseas. Working on the phone with my good friend, Bob Johnson, who was at the auction, I bought the "Lawman" 1970 Boss 429 Mustang, a 1970½ Z28 Trans-Am race-car and a 1968 Yenko Camaro. It was a rush that I'll always remember.

In a world of contrived experiences, the Barrett-Jackson Auction is a genuine shot of adrenaline. I go every year to revel in the automotive lifestyle with fellow car junkies, and sometimes I drive home in the ultimate souvenir.

This book chronicles far more than the evolution of the Barrett-Jackson Auction. It is also an account of the changes that have occurred in collecting cars, which always begins at Barrett-Jackson. I'm honored to be a small part of their story, because everyone who is passionate about cars, or motorcycles or trucks for that matter, owes a debt of gratitude to the people at Barrett-Jackson. They've helped make our dreams come true for the past 35 years.

—Bill Goldberg

PREFACE

Car collecting is quite possibly the most American of all pastimes. The automobile symbolizes the spirit of freedom that has built this country. And ownership of a special muscle car, prewar great classic, hot rod, or sports car allows us to express our individuality and also be part of an exclusive, dedicated group.

While this hobby was once considered the purview of car enthusiasts, the rise to respectability for collectors parallels the growth of the Barrett-Jackson Auction Company. I'm pleased to share that story in this book and the rich history that is the basis for our company.

Barrett-Jackson was founded by two ardent car collectors, Thomas W. Barrett III and my father, Russ Jackson. Tom possessed a wealth of knowledge and had a passion for great prewar, one-off cars from this amazing era. Nearly 10,000 amazing vehicles passed through his hands at one time or another. My father, along with my mother, Nellie, had an affinity for prewar V-16 and V-12 Cadillacs and, of course, the sleek Delahayes.

All of them had a passion for the collector car industry and for the people who are a part of it. This love was passed down to my brother, Brian, and me, and has evolved to include a deep appreciation for muscle cars and the exciting cars being built today.

The Barrett-Jackson team continues to be composed of true "car people" who have grown up restoring cars. We share a passion for the classics, as well as the "next great automobiles" on the market. Some of our team members are former Barrett-Jackson customers, so they understand what fellow aficionados need and want at an auction. This insider knowledge helps us build events each year that enthusiasts enjoy.

The excitement for car collecting that fuels our events is the same passion that I hope you experience while reading this book. That is why I would like to dedicate it to the people who founded this company. I have learned so much from Tom and Russ, who taught me to appreciate and understand every detail of this business. Brian gave me insights that will always be treasured, and my mother is the reason why our solid foundation is intact. She remains the rock and matriarch of our company today.

This book is also a family album, as the automotive lifestyle has been at the center of so much for our clan. Nellie called this chronicle a Barrett-Jackson "love letter" to the car collector industry because we've given our heart and soul to this hobby.

I would be remiss if I did not recognize the extraordinary contributions of the many people who make up the Barrett-Jackson team. From our executive team to the consignment office and everyone who makes our events world-class, your efforts are truly appreciated.

I sincerely hope you enjoy this book, and I appreciate your continued passion. I hope we'll meet again on the block at Barrett-Jackson.

—Craig H. Jackson

Craig Jackson took over the family business and grew it into an automotive lifestyle that extends beyond the collector car community.

INTRODUCTION

"Money is part of it, but passion is what builds collections." Those words are from Alan Lewenthal, whose name may not be immediately recognizable—until I mention that you probably know him as the energetic and animated "Ferrari hat guy" you have seen while watching SPEED's coverage of the Barrett-Jackson Collector Car Auctions in 2005 and 2006.

If I've learned anything while doing interviews and research for this book on the 35th Anniversary of the Barrett-Jackson Collector Car Auction and its showcase event in Scottsdale, Arizona, it's that Lewenthal is right. I'm even tempted to say that he's right on the money. This isn't a book about cars. It is a book about passion. It is not a book about car collecting. It is a book about a lifestyle.

I've spent a lot of time since the conclusion of the 35th Anniversary auction in January 2006 with Craig Jackson, Steve Davis, and others who work in the former Rolls-Royce dealership that serves as Barrett-Jackson's showroom and headquarters. Talking with them reminds me a lot of talking with someone like Giorgetto Guigiaro, the seemingly ageless Italian who has been proclaimed the outstanding automotive designer of all time.

I remember sitting in Guigiaro's office across the Po River from Torino, Italy, asking him a question through an interpreter and listening to him talk for 10 minutes before he broke out into animated laughter. Before I let the interpreter share his answer, I asked her what he was laughing about. "He just realized," she said, "that he's talked for 10 minutes but what he said had nothing to do with answering your question."

But when he finally gave me his answer, I realized immediately that while he may not have provided a direct answer, he had given me wonderful insight to his passion for automobiles and his motivation for designing—decade after decade—many of the world's most cherished vehicles.

Craig Jackson and Steve Davis and others at Barrett-Jackson have that same passion. Ask them a question, and while they generally stay relatively close to the subject, they are quickly overcome by their passion for the people and the cars, and for the changes they are trying to make in the collector car industry and the legacy they hope to leave.

Certainly, as you turn the pages of this book, you'll see the cars and, I hope, learn about Barrett-Jackson auctions and the lifestyle that has grown around them. But more than anything else, I hope you'll also experience the passion that provides the motivation for this automotive extravaganza.

As Craig Jackson puts it: "Passion—this is the heart and the soul of it."

—Larry Edsall

Russ Jackson (left), next to a 1934 LaSalle Convertible, and Tom Barrett, next to a 1936 V-16 Cadillac with body by Hartman, met over a Cadillac that Barrett was selling and that Jackson thought he might buy—but didn't. The sale that didn't happen led to a long relationship and what we now know as the Barrett-Jackson Auction Company. *Photo courtesy of Tom Johnson*

CHAPTER 1

Barrett Meets Jackson

They met over a Cadillac, and not just any Cadillac. Like so many of the cars they would sell through the years, this one had celebrity in its pedigree.

Brian Jackson (left) and his father, Russ, try another sort of horsepower at Arizona's Vista Bonita Ranch, where the Jackson family vacationed for many years before moving from Michigan.

BUT LET'S NOT GET AHEAD of the story. Let's put the transmission in reverse and back up a few years, to the mid-1950s, when *Life* magazine declared that Scottsdale, Arizona, still pretty much a frontier town tucked between Phoenix and the McDowell Mountains, "was one of the most desirable communities in the West."

People paid attention to *Life* magazine in those days, and by 1960, Scottsdale's population swelled to more than 20,000 people. Among the newest of the newcomers that year were the Jacksons and the Barretts.

Russ and Nellie Jackson had been regular vacationers to Scottsdale since the mid-1950s, traveling from Pontiac, Michigan, to spend time at the Vista Bonita Ranch near Pinnacle Peak. The Valley Ho and Camelback Inn were the first of what would become Scottsdale's trademark attractions—resorts and spas—and even then they drew a clientele that included wealthy folks from the East Coast and celebrities from Hollywood.

Nellie Jackson suffered from arthritis and her doctors told her that she'd be much more comfortable living year-round in the warm and dry desert climate. So she, Russ, and their sons, 14-year-old Brian and 1-year-old Craig, moved to Scottsdale in a three-vehicle caravan.

Russ loved cars, especially old Cadillacs with big 12- or 16-cylinder engines. He drove out in a 1934 Cadillac V-12 Opera Coupe that he'd saved from a junkyard. Nellie drove her brand-new 1960 Cadillac. A family friend drove a rented truck that carried the family's nonautomotive possessions.

Russ and Nellie Jackson with their 1925 Locomobile Touring.

Growing up in southeastern Michigan, Russ wanted to be an automotive engineer and had spent three years studying at the General Motors Institute until "calculus got him," as Nellie remembers.

Russ and Nellie met while working in a department store, but she was dismissed when they started dating (a violation of company policy). Russ then convinced Nellie to go to business college. She did, and her first job after graduation was in the cost accounting department at Fisher Body. Ironically, Russ didn't work in the auto industry, but his girlfriend did; General Motors cars may have been badged as Cadillacs, Buicks, Pontiacs, and Chevrolets, but they all had "Body by Fisher" stamped onto the doorsills.

But Nellie's stay at Fisher wasn't long. She was released when she married Russ; company policy banned married women.

Russ had been managing a friend's service station, but now he and Nellie went into their own businesses; hers was a women's clothing store, and his, just down the street from hers, was Russ' Country Store, a general store complete with its own pharmacy and the only license to sell liquor within a five-mile radius.

Once in Scottsdale, Russ and Nellie opened a full-service car wash. They secured a contract to wash Scottsdale's police cars, and they did prep work and car washing for local auto dealerships.

The Jackson family's business roots may have bloomed in the heat of the Southwest desert, but they reach back to Michigan, where Nellie had her own dress shop and where Russ (left) ran a general store and pharmacy.

After moving to Scottsdale, Russ and Nellie opened a full-service car wash. To establish good relations with their new neighbors, they offered to wash Scottsdale's police cars any time they were dirty.

They also started adding to their collection of Cadillacs. Soon after arriving in Scottsdale, Russ bought a 1953 Cadillac Derham limousine from the owner of the Superstition Inn, a resort in nearby Mesa complete with its own Western movie set. Elvis Presley stayed at the Inn while shooting *Charro!*, and the television series *Have Gun, Will Travel* was filmed on the set. Series star Richard Boone, who played gun-for-hire Paladin, often rode from the airport to the hotel in the limo.

IT IS ESTIMATED, CONSERVATIVELY AT THAT, THAT SOME 10,000 CARS— INCLUDING MANY OF THE MOST VALUABLE CLASSIC CARS IN THE WORLD—PASSED THROUGH TOM BARRETT'S HANDS, SOME OF THEM FIVE OR EVEN SIX TIMES.

Nellie Jackson poses with the 1953 Cadillac Derham limousine that annually carried the family back to Michigan to visit friends and family. Nellie remembers using the privacy window so she and Russ could drive without hearing their noisy sons.

For the Jacksons, the limo became their daily driver, serving their family much as subsequent generations would use minivans and sport utility vehicles. Nellie remembers their annual drive back to Michigan, and how they'd put the boys in the back and raise the privacy window so she and Russ could enjoy the trip in peace and quiet.

ARRIVING IN SCOTTSDALE JUST A MONTH AFTER THE JACKSONS were Tom W. Barrett III, his wife, Bonnie, and their four children. Barrett was the son of a federal judge and had grown up in Oak Park, Illinois, just outside Chicago. Like Russ Jackson, cars were Tom Barrett's passion, and he had started collecting them while still a teenager. Barrett also was involved in real estate, and he soon discovered that car collectors were good customers when it was time to wheel and deal for a vintage vehicle or a piece of property.

It is estimated, conservatively at that, that some 10,000 cars—including many of the most valuable classic cars in the world—passed through Tom Barrett's hands, some of them five or even six times. Many consider Barrett the grandfather of the car-collecting hobby. Indeed, the Classic Car Club of America named the building that houses its own collection at Michigan's Gilmore Car Museum in Tom Barrett's honor.

But again, we're getting ahead of the story. Back to Scottsdale in the early 1960s . . .

Spectators take a close look at the cars at one of the early *Fiesta de los Autos Elegantes*.

A couple of months after arriving in Scottsdale, Tom Barrett placed an advertisement to sell a 1933 16-cylinder Cadillac Town Car he'd acquired. This was no ordinary '33 Caddy. This one-of-a-kind car had been built for Hollywood movie star Joan Crawford and reportedly stole the show when she arrived in it at the Academy Awards that year.

Always passionate about big-engined Caddys, Russ Jackson was very interested, and so Jackson met with Barrett.

While they didn't strike a deal for the Crawford Cadillac—in fact, Nellie Jackson remembers, Russ never did buy a car from Tom Barrett—they established a car-based friendship that by 1967 found their families working together to stage the *Fiesta de los Auto Elegantes*, a car show and parade held to raise money for Scottsdale's art center and to buy books for the community's library.

Vehicles with celebrity provenance and raising money for charities would become important building blocks in the Barrett and Jackson families' future business endeavors.

A program cover from one of the *Fiesta de los Autos Elegantes*, the car show Russ Jackson and Tom Barrett staged as a fundraiser for Scottsdale charities, including the community's art center.

Tom Barrett receives the "Miss Classy Chassis" award in 1968 when his V-16 Cadillac Phaeton was named best in show at the *Fiesta de los Autos Elegantes*.

Nine-year-old Craig Jackson poses with his 1939 Austin Bantam and the trophy it won. This was Craig's first car, although he was too young to have a license to drive it on public streets.

A 1917 Pierce-Arrow with Russ Jackson at the wheel.

Mrs. and Governor Jack Williams with Russ Jackson in the late 1960s.

The "highlight" of one of the early *Fiesta de los Autos Elegantes* came when a 1931 Cadillac All-weather Phaeton V-12 caught fire during the parade. Below is how the car looked after it was restored to number one condition after the fire.

Since 1989, the Barrett-Jackson Auction has been at WestWorld, a horseshow and event center in Scottsdale, which is only 10 miles north from the original auction site.

CHAPTER 2

The Barrett-Jackson Collector Car Auction Is Born

Tom Barrett and Russ Jackson staged their last Fiesta de los Auto Elegantes car show in the fall of 1971 and immediately started working on a collector car auction to be held at the end of December.

BARRETT AND JACKSON SEEDED THE FIELD with 75 vehicles from their personal collections, but Barrett's 50 cars and Jackson's 25 represented only half of those offered at the sale, held next to the Safari Resort on Scottsdale Road, the community's main street.

Tom Barrett was a showman, a wheeler-dealer who operated in the tradition of P. T. Barnum, and arrangements were made for the sale of the auction's star vehicles—Barrett's pair of Mercedes-Benz 770 Phaetons, former Adolf Hitler staff cars (one from Berlin, the other from Berchtesgaden)—to be reported live on the national weekend evening news, with commentary from Roger Mudd at the anchor desk in New York City.

Accommodating television meant pushing up the auction schedule by an hour, but the adjustment proved more than worthwhile. One of the Phaetons sold for more than $90,000, and the other set a world-record collector car price of $153,000. The size of the sale and its national television coverage brought invaluable attention to the first Barrett-Jackson Auction.

Boosted by the Phaetons, that first Barrett-Jackson Auction posted $650,000 in sales, although Craig Jackson remembers that while the auction included Duesenbergs, Packards, Cadillacs, and the Mercedes, many of the cars were simply restored Model A Fords—though there were several very nice Woodys that still had their original wood panels intact.

Ironically, it was the cars in the parking lot of that first—and other early Barrett-Jackson Auctions—that would become highly sought-after collector cars more than three decades later. These were muscle cars including Chevrolet Chevelles and Plymouth HEMI 'Cudas that in the early 1970s were the daily drivers for car enthusiasts.

Tom Barrett brought the auction company national media coverage when he sold both of his Mercedes-Benz 770 Phaetons that were built for the Third Reich and used for all their leaders.

It's a Duesy! The beauty of the cars built by the Duesenberg brothers was so startling that the expression became part of the American lexicon.

A Delahaye displays the combination of luxury fittings and voluptuous bodywork that makes such examples of rolling sculpture so attractive to car collectors.

A car didn't have to come from France to be glamorous. Here's a made-in-America 1937 Lincoln.

Bugatti remains a magic name among car collectors. This is a 1934 Type 51, a race car.

That's a young Craig Jackson sitting at the steering wheel of a 1927 Rolls-Royce which he had just restored.

French automaker Delage made its name in racing, but also produced highly collectible cars for the road as well.

An aerial view of the 1981 Barrett-Jackson Auction held at Phoenix Municipal Stadium.

The second Barrett-Jackson Auction again took place in the lot next to the Safari Resort. However, by 1977, the event had outgrown that location and was moved to Phoenix Municipal Stadium, a baseball complex constructed in 1966 for Cactus League spring training exhibition games. In the auction's second year at Phoenix, 800 cars crossed the block and those sold brought in $4 million.

By 1989, an even larger venue was needed. The auction moved back home to Scottsdale, to an equestrian facility known as HorseWorld. While the facility's name later changed to a less equestrian-sounding WestWorld, the site nonetheless retained its primary focus on Scottsdale's important international role with another kind of horsepower—polo fields and horse show facilities.

Among those who preferred mechanical horsepower, cars from the 1950s were starting to become popular with collectors, many of whom grew up in those postwar years and had fond memories of big-finned Cadillacs and Chrysler letter-series cars. Still, the classics from the 1930s remained the primary attraction at Barrett-Jackson. In 1987, former Indianapolis 500–winning car owner Andy Granatelli became the first person to pay more than $1 million for a collector car at the Barrett-Jackson Auction when he purchased a 1932 Duesenberg Model J Derham Tourister.

Andy Granatelli has his right arm around Gordon Behring, designer of the 1932 Duesenberg Model J Derham Tourister. The former Indy 500 car–owner had just purchased the car for more than $1 million at the 1987 Barrett-Jackson Auction.

In 1990, a 1932 Hispano-Suiza J12 Binder and a 1938 Bugatti Type 57S Atalante went for more than $2 million each at Barrett-Jackson. That auction drew 60,000 spectators, and the $37.3 million in total sales established a Barrett-Jackson record that would stand until 2004.

One reason it took a while for that record to fall was that the very nature of car collecting was changing—and not necessarily for the better. Foreign money and gold-chained speculators looking to turn a quick profit were operating as "day traders," driving up prices—especially on exotic European sports cars—but they were also driving away many genuine car collectors who simply were being priced out of the hobby.

At that 1990 Barrett-Jackson Auction, a matched set of 1973 Ferrari Daytonas, one a Berlinetta (coupe) and the other a Spyder (roadster), sold for an astounding $2.2 million.

Within the next two years, that inflationary, speculator-blown bubble would burst, and it would take a few years for the car-collecting hobby to find a new equilibrium, once again based on real economic terms of supply and demand among car collectors. And by the time that finally happened, almost nothing would remain the same.

WITHIN THE NEXT TWO YEARS, THAT INFLATIONARY, SPECULATOR-BLOWN BUBBLE WOULD BURST, AND IT WOULD TAKE A FEW YEARS FOR THE CAR-COLLECTING HOBBY TO FIND A NEW EQUILIBRIUM.

Classic car collectors cherish cars this 1939 Packard Darrin Victoria, that epitomize the pinnacle of American car building in the pre-war era.

Packard produced large and luxurious cars for wealthy Americans and they have remained prized by car collectors. This is a 1931 Packard Modified 745.

A 1934 La Salle was a car that would draw a lot of attention in the early years of the Barrett-Jackson auctions.

This 1932 Packard 902 Club Sedan brought $87,400 at the Barrett-Jackson Auction in 2004.

Live coverage of the Barrett-Jackson auction has turned Craig Jackson and many of his cutomers into sought-after television personalities.

CHAPTER 3

Craig Comes of Age

The 1990s were a decade of transition for the Barrett-Jackson Auction Company. And by the time that finally happened, almost nothing would remain the same.

AFTER A LONG BOUT with colon cancer, Russ Jackson died in 1993. His oldest son, Brian, had been managing the company, but then Brian took ill while attending the Pebble Beach Concours d'Elegance in summer 1995. Six weeks later, Brian Jackson died—at age 49—of the same disease that had claimed his father.

"My dad died the day after the auction in 1993," Craig Jackson remembers. "We knew it was coming, but it was still hard. But when my brother got sick at Pebble Beach and died six weeks later...

"That first year that I took over was tough," he continues. "Burying my brother. Getting his estate in order. The politics in the company. We were in disagreement at that time with the Barretts about the way we conducted the auction, the type of cars, sticking to our corporate policy. Tom Barrett was ready to retire and we ended up buying them out."

Brian Jackson was in charge of the Barrett-Jackson Auction Company but died unexpectedly in 1995 after a brief fight against cancer.

As if all of that wasn't enough for the company's new leader, he realized that "the consigners were calling the shots. The [collector car] dealers were controlling a lot of things." Jackson remembers how cars would be consigned for auction, and advertised by Barrett-Jackson, only to be sold privately before the auction opened. "It wasn't fair and even for everybody," he said, angry at how such maneuvers were hurting the reputation of his family's business.

Brian (left) and Craig Jackson join auctioneer Andy Adcock on the stand.

Jackson knew that for the company to grow "we had to make our experience better for our customers."

Craig had ideas of how to do that. In fact, he and his older brother, Brian, had often talked about ways to enhance what they saw as the "Barrett-Jackson experience." They'd actually begun that effort in 1995 by signing Chrysler as the first presenting sponsor of the Barrett-Jackson Auction. Chrysler celebrated its sponsorship with a massive display of its vehicles at the WestWorld venue, and not just vehicles available at Chrysler Group dealerships. Many of the company's most historic vehicles, such as the d'Elegance concept car, the De Soto Adventurer concept, a Firearrow roadster, one of only 50 turbine-powered cars built in the 1960s, as well as a 1971 HEMI 'Cuda convertible, and three of the prototypes used to develop the Viper were on display at the 1995 auction.

Still, with the 1996 Barrett-Jackson Auction just a few months off, Craig spent a lot with Brian at his house. "I asked him what to do."

"You know what to do. You always knew what to do. Do it," Brian told his younger brother.

"I asked him a lot of questions that day. 'Should I do this?' 'Should I do that?'" Craig remembers, taking a moment to wipe tears from his eyes. That was a hard day.

He said, 'Believe in yourself, take care of your daughter and our mother, and do the right thing.'"

Craig also got approval, "the nod" as he puts it, from his mother, Nellie, who has been closely involved in the family business from the very beginning and who, even in her 80s, is usually the first person to arrive each morning at the Barrett-Jackson offices. "She provided a great foundation," Craig says. "She gave me the nod to do what was best."

What was best, Craig determined, was to make the auction experience better for Barrett-Jackson's customers, and to grow the customer base by making the collector car hobby accessible to more people, especially to a baby-boomer generation that was quickly reaching the point where its own children were leaving the nest, leaving the boomers with money to spend on something other than orthodontics, college tuition, or their daughters' weddings.

"I wanted to turn Barrett-Jackson into a lifestyle experience, something that was a destination, which the auction was, but to expand on that," he says. "I wanted it to be a lifestyle event that you have to go to, like SEMA [the Specialty Equipment Market Association's annual show, which is closed to the public but a must-attend event for automakers and others in the industry. Formerly just an aftermarket trade show, SEMA has become a place where new cars are launched, where clients are entertained, and where major deals are done].

"I wanted to change the perception that Barrett-Jackson is just an auction. It's more than that. It's a car *show*. The auction is the epicenter, and provides the drama, but there needed to be many different components."

> "I WANTED TO CHANGE THE PERCEPTION THAT BARRETT-JACKSON IS JUST AN AUCTION. IT'S MORE THAN THAT. IT'S A CAR SHOW."
> —CRAIG JACKSON

Nellie and Russ Jackson at the 1985 Pebble Beach Concours d'Elegance with their Invicta, a car featured in *Motor Trend* magazine. *Photo courtesy of Bob Coffman aka FotoBob*

To put Craig's goal into language a car collector understands, he wanted to do nothing short of a ground-up restoration—and not just of Barrett-Jackson but of the entire car-collecting hobby.

CRAIG JACKSON HAD GROWN UP not just in the auction company, but in the car-collecting hobby. He was 12 years old when the first Barrett-Jackson Auction was held. Even in the early 1970s, he was put in charge of parking and of the drivers who shuttled the auction cars back and forth around the grounds—and it didn't matter to anyone that at the time Craig was still too young to have a driver's license of his own.

Brian Jackson works on the restoration of a Hispano-Suiza V-12 engine.

"We had fifteen hundred cars in three lots and I organized all that," he remembers. "I took on all the opportunities I could to be involved in the operations, in building the site, especially when we went to Phoenix Municipal Stadium."

But auction operations weren't Craig Jackson's only interest. While many see the head of the Barrett-Jackson Company as a gregarious, type A personality—and he is—he's also quite the computer geek and has been writing programs in various computer languages for many years.

Craig Jackson (left) and his older brother, Brian, work on the restoration of an Auburn Boatail.

"I started trying to computerize things," he recalls. "I took on what was the start of our IT department in 1985. We computerized our accounting, and then on to the Internet and into desktop and then digital publishing."

Far right: **A teenage Craig Jackson sands a 1973 Corvette.**

But before he was learning about accounting programs and Quark publishing software, Craig Jackson was learning to appreciate a variety of cars, and was getting

his hands dirty—not to mention scraped up, even wounded—working in the family's restoration shop.

"I grew up hanging out with my brother and buddies," Craig remembers. "There was a fourteen-year age difference and Brian got stuck baby-sitting me."

Baby-sitting by big brother meant that Craig spent a lot of time at Bee Line Dragway, or cruising Central Avenue through downtown Phoenix, or going down to Brian's race shop on 56th Street and Washington, where Brian and his buddies worked on their cars.

"I grew up with him and his buddies around a lot of great muscle cars and race cars," Craig remembers. "They drove Camaros and 'Cudas and all of those kinds of cars. I really had a love affair with those kinds of cars."

And around the turn of the twenty-first century, so would the entire car-collecting world.

But muscle cars weren't the only cars in which Craig Jackson had developed a passion.

Through his father's business partner, Tom Barrett, he'd grown up around many of the world's finest classic cars—Duesenbergs, Packards, Mercedes, Rolls-Royces—and especially the one-offs for which Barrett searched the world to add to his collection. Jackson's father loved those big-engined prewar Cadillacs and the "French classics," the coachbuilt cars by Figoni and Falaschi, Saoutchik, and others who combined artistic design and craftsmanship.

"My brother was a true baby boomer," Craig adds. "He graduated in the early 1960s, right around the era of *American Graffiti*." Craig also remembers his brother's fondness for drag cars of that era, and that Brian was among the first to become involved in vintage sports car racing when in the mid-1970s Steve Earle realized it was time for old race cars to come out of barns and back onto the track.

Craig Jackson works on a slant-nose Porsche that he restored. Craig also built special slant-nose kits for other Porsche 911 owners.

Top: **The slant nose after Craig Jackson's restoration.**

A 1939 Bugatti Saoutchik.

Former Grand Prix racing champion and well-known car restoration expert Phil Hill joins Brian Jackson at the Stardust Raceway.

From such a background, Craig was able to hone his own automotive interests.

"Tom and Russ and my brother each liked different things," he says. "I liked performance and style and durability."

For Craig, that meant muscle cars, sports cars, and those French classics.

"I don't necessarily share the passion for as many of the big 'classics'," he admits. "I've worked on them. I've driven them. I guess I'm a little tainted, because I've been in most of the world's great classics, and some of them are more fantasy than reality. They have no synchros. They are just work to drive. French cars, on the other hand, you have Cotal gearboxes. You have wild coachwork. They're fun to drive."

Jackson's appreciation for French cars motivated him to invest 10,000 hours of his own time in restoring a 1948 Figoni and Falachi–bodied Delahaye that his parents bought in the early 1980s on a trip to Europe. They saw that the car was for sale, but the owner was not available so they left word that they were interested.

"We came home and Russ got a call the next day from the owner," says Nellie Jackson. "Russ flew back the next day and bought the car."

The car arrived in Phoenix in a shipping crate. Inside were boxes, none of them more than two feet tall. "Where's the car?" Craig wondered when the crate was opened. It was inside those boxes, in pieces, he discovered.

"There was a lot more than some assembly required," he says, laughing in retrospect. "They had disassembled everything, including the engine and transmission."
Craig had to create new wooden chassis pieces and redo most of the car's metal body. With the exception of the car's interior, he did all the work himself.

"My goal was to prove that I could do a car from ground up to one hundred points," he recalls, proud to say that in 1987, at the Classic Car of America Grand Classic, the Delahaye earned a perfect 100-point score.

THE DELAHAYE MAY HAVE REPRESENTED Craig Jackson's best work in the restoration shop, but it certainly was not his first such effort. He had been building up to this moment since he was in high school.

"My dad never really—and I'm trying to instill this in my children—he never really spoiled me," says Craig Jackson. "Actually, he did the opposite. He made me work for everything.

"I wanted a dirt bike but he wouldn't buy me one because he figured I was going to kill myself—and he was probably pretty close. I got a paper route and worked as a busboy and did the jobs in the shop that my brother didn't want to do. But I learned how to work an English wheel and how to block sand and to pick and file and all of those things from a bunch of old guys who

When his father bought this 1948 Figoni and Falachi–bodied Delahaye, it arrived in Scottsdale in pieces. Craig Jackson had to do more than simply restore the car—he had to re-create much of the chrome.

were still around. And my dad cut me a deal. I was a junior in high school and I was driving my grandmother's 1966 Pontiac Le Mans—that was my first car, and I still have it—and I proceeded to put a hot cam and other stuff in it and I just beat the heck out of it.

"I wanted a 1969 Z28 [Chevrolet Camaro] and my dad made a deal with me: If I made the principal's list, he'd go shopping with me for a [used] Z28. I made the list and we looked at three or four Camaros, and every one of them, you'd shut the door and they'd rattle."

Craig Jackson's first car was this 1966 Pontiac Le Mans, which had been his grandmother's car. Craig did some considerable tweaking of the car, a vehicle he still owns.

This is the 1968 Corvette that Craig Jackson restored while still in high school.

Although he wanted a Camaro when they'd struck the deal, high schooler Craig's tastes were changing, and what he wanted now was a Chevrolet Corvette. After looking at and rejecting several Camaros, Craig convinced his father to see what 'Vettes might be available.

"We looked at one near the Arizona State University campus, a '68 Corvette, 427, T-Top, Le Mans blue, and it's just clapped out. I looked at it for about ten seconds. It was a pretty rough beast, so I blew it off and went back to our truck," Craig remembers. "But I turned around and saw my dad shaking the guy's hand!

'What are you doing?' Craig asked when he got to his father's side.

'Oh,' Russ said, 'I bought it. I think it will be a good summer project for you.' "

Even as a soon-to-be-senior in high school, Craig had learned enough as an apprentice in the shop to take on the Corvette's resurrection. He rebuilt the engine and transmission and seemingly everything on the car. "It was the first car I actually did all one-hundred percent myself, and looking back it was a good experience and really started me on my way."

JUST AS FACING AN UNEXPECTED REBUILD on the Corvette established Craig Jackson's skills in car restoration, facing an unexpected role as the rebuilder of the Barrett-Jackson Auction established Craig Jackson's skills as a visionary businessman who was not only changing his own company, but was turning the collector car hobby into an entertainment industry.

As Craig Jackson moved into the leadership role at Barrett-Jackson, Roger Werner, one of the founders of ESPN, cable television's 24-hours-a-day all-sports network, was starting a new enterprise, Speedvision. The Financial News Network had televised part of the Barrett-Jackson Auction, and Werner was among those watching. Speedvision would be devoted to motorsports, automobiles, motorcycles, and the like, and Werner and Jackson struck a deal to tape the 1996 Barrett-Jackson Auction for viewing on the fledgling channel.

The coverage was such a hit that the following year Speedvision provided six hours of live auction coverage. By the 2006 Barrett-Jackson Auction, SPEED (as it is now known) would broadcast 34 hours of live auction coverage, which had become what SPEED's top executive, executive vice president and general manager Hunter Nickell, called a "ratings juggernaut."

Television exposed car collecting to a much wider audience, and would eventually turn some bidders into car-collecting celebrities. But there was another change that Craig Jackson was making that would reverberate through the car-collecting industry.

Traditionally, when cars—or other items, for that matter—are offered at auction, they come with a reserve, an unpublished dollar amount set by the seller. If no bid exceeds the reserve, the item is retained by the seller. It was bad enough if the item didn't sell after taking time on the block. Even worse, however, was what the auction companies call being "curbed"—when the seller sets a high reserve, watches the bidding, and then, after the car doesn't meet its reserve, goes out to the curb and makes a private sale to one of those bidders.

Craig Jackson co-hosted the *Autoclassics* program on the Financial News Network in 1994.

To Craig Jackson, "the tail was wagging the dog."

To spectators watching in the tent or on television, no sale meant no excitement.

Craig Jackson knew he had a tough decision to make. But he also knew that "Brian and I had talked about it. It needed to happen. We weren't going to have bidding on a car just for a guy to get himself an appraisal."

Barrett-Jackson already had a policy of trying to make sure that one-third of the cars offered at its auction were offered with No Reserve. To more strongly encourage consigners to offer cars with no strings attached, Craig manipulated the auction docket, saving coveted spots in the prime-time television coverage for vehicles offered without the shadow of a secret minimum acceptable price.

Mike Joy is a veteran member of SPEED's team who provides analysis of the Barrett-Jackson Auction.

Craig Jackson (left) recruited long-time customer Steve Davis to become executive vice president of the Barrett-Jackson Auction Company.

The old guard wasn't happy. "If it's not broken, don't fix it" was their feeling. Craig's idea was: "If I don't think we can sell your car at the reserve you want, we're not going to take the car."

And, he adds, "When the cards are stacked against me, I don't retreat. I don't just go pout and cry. I get tough and suck it up and deal with it."

Jackson found allies in two of what he considered to be Barrett-Jackson's best customers, two men who were both consigners and buyers: Gary Bennett of Tulsa, Oklahoma, and Steve Davis of Valley Oak Auto in Visalia, California. Both would eventually join the Barrett-Jackson team on a full-time basis.

Bennett was an architect and car collector. Jackson recalls that in 1999, when high winds cracked a couple of the poles supporting the auction tent, Bennett grabbed a sledgehammer and was pounding support stakes into the ground so the auction could resume when the poles were repaired. "He's a customer and he was pounding stakes," Jackson says. "There's a friend."

Gary Bennett was another Barrett-Jackson Auction customer recruited by Craig Jackson to work full-time for the company.

After Bennett retired from his business, Jackson hired him in summer 2002 as senior automotive specialist, the person who verifies—as much as possible—the pedigree of every car offered for auction (the same job Craig Jackson had when his brother was running the company).

Meanwhile, Davis had discovered that his cars sold very well at Barrett-Jackson when he offered them at No Reserve, in part because he worked hard to make sure bidders knew all the details of his cars' histories and the work that went into their maintenance or restoration. Davis was president of the Visalia Motorsports Festival, a 501(c)3 California corporation that organized the Pan-Pacific road race, a re-creation of one of the first American auto races, and led the effort to keep California from destroying collector cars when the state passed stiff auto pollution regulations. Jackson eventually hired Davis to become senior executive vice president of Barrett-Jackson, in charge of all automotive aspects of the auction, including car selection and scheduling, and also settling any disagreements that might arise involving sellers or buyers.

IN 1995, ABOUT 700 CARS CROSSED THE AUCTION BLOCK at Barrett-Jackson. In 1996, Craig Jackson's first year in charge, that number dropped to fewer than 600.

"But we sold a higher percentage. We actually sold more cars," Craig Jackson remembers. "And we grossed more money."

The 1995 auction took in $14 million, but only 430 of 700 cars were actually sold. In 1996, 396 cars sold—68 percent of those offered—for a total of $16.4 million.

Encouraged by the response to his changes, Craig Jackson went even further for the 1997 auction. His goal: Turn a collector car auction into an entertainment destination that would appeal not just to car guys, but to their wives and families as well.

"We advertised the cars and the experience of coming to Scottsdale, of experiencing everything we have to offer, and of coming to make it a weekend," Craig Jackson says. "That changed not just Barrett-Jackson, but I think our whole industry, from just an old boys club of collecting old cars to something that was more accepted."

To give wives something to do while their husbands were watching cars go over the block, Barrett-Jackson had a different set of models—fashion models—walking the runway, and there were charity events and a variety of vendors selling everything from automotive art to fashionable furs.

To enhance the auction's appeal to those who couldn't come to Scottsdale, SPEED offered live coverage, and now even those sitting at home could bid on the cars over the Barrett-Jackson website.

Sales topped $15 million, again with about 65 percent of cars offered actually selling. But the impact of the changes was becoming more clearly evident the following year. In 1998, not only did 65 percent of the 702 vehicles sell—totaling more than $17 million—but more than 115,000 people attended the Barrett-Jackson Auction.

And the growth continued. In 1999, attendance jumped to 125,000, and 77 percent of 800 vehicles offered sold for a combined $22 million. Another element was added to the auction, too: a four-day collector car road rally that finished as the auction began.

Craig Jackson shakes hands with Prince Albert of Monaco. Barrett-Jackson staged the *Legende et Passion* auction in Monte Carlo as part of the Historic Grand Prix weekend in 2000.

Craig Jackson drives a 300 SL Mercedes around the grand prix course at Monaco.

Top right: **Vintage grand prix cars race in the Historic Grand Prix at Monte Carlo in 2000.**

Craig Jackson continued to experiment with ways to expand not only the Scottsdale auction, but the Barrett-Jackson Auction experience. In 2000, Barrett-Jackson went to Monaco for its first overseas auction, *Legende et Passion*, as part of the Historic Grand Prix. A year later, Barrett-Jackson held a Father's Day weekend auction at the Petersen Museum in Los Angeles, where the Batmobile from the movie *Batman Returns* sold for $175,000.

However, the addition of a second event to the auction company's schedule really didn't blossom until 2003, when Barrett-Jackson—encouraged by Manheim Auto Auctions, which auctions off late-model cars to dealers—staged a collector car auction in Palm Beach, Florida.

In 2001, the Batmobile from the movie *Batman Returns* sold for $175,000 at a Father's Day weekend auction staged by Barrett-Jackson at the Petersen Museum in Los Angeles.

There are socioeconomic similarities between Scottsdale and Palm Beach, but even Craig Jackson is amazed that the Florida auction has done as well as it has: $6 million in sales the first year, $11.8 million the second, $22 million the third, and $35 million by 2006, where the action was so furious on Saturday night that SPEED stayed with the bidding for 49 minutes without diverting its coverage for a commercial.

"KIDS ARE BIDDING WITH THEIR DADS," HE SAYS. "EIGHT- AND TEN-YEAR-OLDS ALREADY ARE INTO THE HOBBY, BECAUSE THEY'VE BEEN WATCHING ON SPEED FOR SEVERAL YEARS."

—CRAIG JACKSON

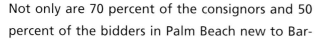

Not only are 70 percent of the consignors and 50 percent of the bidders in Palm Beach new to Barrett-Jackson, Craig Jackson notes, but he's seen an entirely new phenomenon at the Florida venue: "Kids are bidding with their dads," he says. "Eight- and ten-year-olds already are into the hobby, because they've been watching on SPEED Channel for several years."

Left: **Carroll Shelby thanks Craig Jackson for throwing a terrific 80th birthday party.** *Courtesy of Stanton Photography*

What looks like a Shelby Cobra is actually a birthday cake. The opening-night gala for the 2003 Barrett-Jackson Auction was transformed into an 80th birthday celebration for automotive legend Carroll Shelby. *Courtesy of Stanton Photography*

BARRETT-JACKSON CELEBRATED ITS 30TH ANNIVERSARY IN 2001 with 150,000 people attending its Scottsdale auction, where a record 83 percent of the vehicles sold for a total of $26.7 million. The following year a record 87 percent of nearly 800 cars sold for $26.9 million, and SPEED increased live coverage to 10 hours of action.

Sales topped 90 percent and reached nearly $29 million in 2003, when 175,000 people turned out for a Scottsdale auction that truly had become an automotive lifestyle "experience" with 5,000 people on hand for an opening-night gala that doubled as an 80th birthday party for automotive and motorsports legend Carroll Shelby. The auction itself was held in a 140,000-square-foot tent. Between the cars and about 300 on-site vendors and exhibitors, the action covered 360 acres.

In the big tent, a 1967 Ford Mustang Shelby GT500 E (Eleanor) fastback sold for $194,400, a 1966 Shelby Cobra 427 got $253,800, and a 1967 Ford GT40 Mark I race car—again with Shelby heritage—garnered nearly $350,000. The action was spirited as actors Don Johnson and Cheech Marin were on hand to encourage bidders who ran the 1970 Plymouth 'Cuda convertible from the *Nash Bridges* television show up to nearly $150,000. Outselling all of them, however, was a 1957 Jaguar XKSS roadster that went for $1.1 million.

Helping to celebrate Carroll Shelby's birthday are racers Dan Gurney, Bob Bondurant, and Parnelli Jones, and Craig Jackson. *Courtesy of Stanton Photography*

SPEED increased live coverage to 15 hours for 2004, with cameras on hand for all four days of an auction that drew more than 760 cars—with more than 744 of them selling at a record-setting rate of 98 percent. Attendance topped 185,000. Sales totaled more than $38.5 million, and the highest price was $432,000, but it was not made on a classic or even a muscle car, but on a 1938 Lincoln Zephyr V-12 street rod. It appeared that Craig Jackson's overhaul of not only his own auction but of the entire collector car industry was just about complete.

"Now there were numerous reasons for a lot of different people to come to Scottsdale," he notes. "We used to run straight classics in a row on Saturday, and if you didn't care about classics, you left. But now it's all mixed up. Now you don't now whether to go look at the cars or the vendors or the sponsor displays or the driving track. The auction's still the core, but if the car you're into isn't going on the block for a couple of

This 1957 Jaguar XKSS sold for more than $1.1 million at the Barrett-Jackson Auction in 2003.

Craig Jackson (in the driver's seat), Steve Davis (kneeling), and Gary Bennett are on camera for an episode of *Car Search*.

hours, there are lots of other things to do. And with the Jumbotrons, people can pay attention to what's going on in the arena without actually having to be in the tent."

AS AMAZING AS THE NUMBERS WERE IN 2004, Craig Jackson and his crew were far from finished. Together with SPEED, Barrett-Jackson did a 26-episode "reality" behind-the-scenes television series—*Barrett-Jackson Car Search*—with teams of collectors scouring their areas for cars they bought, prepared, and then sold at Barrett-Jackson. The program had done its job, so Barrett-Jackson and SPEED next presented *Life on the Block,* a series that provided a behind-the-scenes look at the auction through the eyes of leading consigners and bidders. Like *Car Search, Life* provided an entertaining look at car collecting and enhanced the education of newcomers to the hobby.

Off-season television shows had their purpose, but Craig Jackson's biggest accomplishment for the 2005 Barrett-Jackson Auction was finally achieving the dream of an entire event with all vehicles—all 871 of them—offered at No Reserve.

"The bidders realized that the cars were actually going to sell," Craig Jackson says. "It's evolved to where people know they can buy the cars."

But not even Craig Jackson or Steve Davis—with their ability to manipulate the order of the auction, with their ability to add a fifth day to the auction, with SPEED offering 24 hours of live coverage—could have anticipated what would happen at WestWorld in January 2005.

Craig Jackson's very own 1970 Plymouth HEMI 'Cuda convertible was featured on *Car Search*.

Even before the auction began, the annual gala opened the auction week that would generate more than $1.75 million for charities, such as Childhelp USA, with all proceeds going to the charities and with Barrett-Jackson waiving its usual commissions.

As the auction unfolded, muscle cars were bringing very healthy prices. On Thursday, a 1969 Oldsmobile 4-4-2 convertible reached $105,840. Early in the day on Friday, muscle cars, Shelby Mustangs, and Corvettes were drawing strong six-figure bids. That evening, a 1961 Chrysler 300 G convertible, given only routine notice in the auction catalog, reached $205,200; a 1970 Plymouth HEMI 'Cuda coupe went for just shy of $300,000.

Saturday afternoon got rocking with a 1970 'Cuda coupe bringing $329,000, a 1955 Chevrolet "resto mod"—a car with a stock-appearing body and anything but stock

mechanical components (consider its 600-horsepower V-8 engine)—hitting $221,400. A 1952 Allard J2X roadster and a 1947 Ford Woody custom went for similar numbers, and then a new Ford GT, a 1957 Mercedes 300SL roadster, Boyd Coddington's *Chezoom* (a custom based on a 1957 Chevrolet Bel Air), and a 1970 Chevrolet Chevelle convertible were each well over $300,000.

The pump had been primed for prime time, and now the star of the auction, the golden-colored 1954 Oldsmobile F-88 concept car, created by Harley Earl and his design department for the General Motors Motorama show, rolled onto the stage.

Though the car was far from the star of Motorama that year, it certainly had a fascinating history.

Long before there were major international auto shows, there was General Motors Motorama, an event engineered by GM design director Harley Earl to showcase his ideas for America's automotive future. Earl had invented the concept car in the 1930s. By the 1950s, his studios were producing a succession of such dream machines.

At the 2005 Barrett-Jackson Auction, this 1961 Chrysler 300 G received only routine mention in the catalog, yet sold for $205,200 during a Friday night bidding frenzy.

Most of them, however, were destined for destruction, though a few escaped the scrap yard. The Olds F-88, basically a Chevrolet Corvette with Oldsmobile-style bodywork, was among those that survived, primarily, it seems, because Earl liked it enough that he used it for his daily driver, and then shipped it off to California, to his friend and former automaker E. L. Cord.

Through the years, the F-88 would have a dozen different owners. Indeed, it was sold three times previously at Barrett-Jackson, most recently in 1997 to Gordon Apker, a car collector from Seattle. Apker has a philosophy that if he hasn't driven a car in two years, he sells it, so the Oldsmobile concept was back at Barrett-Jackson in 2005, and it was significant enough that it was one of eight cars featured on the cover of the auction's 218-page catalog.

We were about to see that critical mass had been achieved in the car-collecting world. It took maybe 10 minutes for the F-88 to sell, but as *AutoWeek* magazine reported, "It was perhaps the most emotional 10 minutes of automotive television in recent history."

Craig Jackson figured that in the current car-collecting market, the F-88 might fetch as much as three-quarters of a million dollars. Almost immediately the bidding reached $550,000, and Allan Jones, a collector from Tennessee, was waiting for the gavel to drop and the car to be his.

In 1954, this Oldsmobile F-88 concept car was built for General Motors' Motorama. As recently as 1997, it had been sold at Barrett-Jackson for a fraction of the 2005 price.

Bidder assistant Amy Sparks Assiter works with bidder Allan Jones.

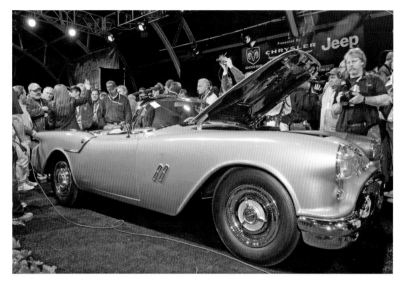

But then the "Ferrari hat guy" got into the action. Alan Lewenthal was curator of the Gateway Auto Museum, a facility being built in western Colorado by John Hendricks, founder of Discovery Communications and thus of more than a dozen cable television networks. Hendricks wanted the museum to showcase the finest in American automotive history, and he and Lewenthal had come to Barrett-Jackson on a shopping spree.

"The car needs to be in a museum, not in a private collection," Lewenthal said.

Even Craig Jackson was stunned at the drama that unfolded into a bidding battle for the historic Oldsmobile concept car.

Lewenthal's bid—as well as his emotional enthusiasm on the block—set a spark that swept through the tent. "That guy that day provided the most amazing action I'd ever seen," said a stunned Craig Jackson.

Quickly, the bidding hit $1 million, and it did that without Jones, who figured the car was worth $600,000 and had stopped at that point. But then Lewenthal challenged him, "provoked me," is how Jones put it, "so I got back in at a million three."

Other bidders—as many as seven people were bidding on the car—backed off at $1.6 million, leaving Lewenthal and a car collector from the Phoenix area to go toe to toe.

"I'm serious," Lewenthal said as he bid $2 million.

So was his antagonist, who took the bidding to $2.7 million.

Lewenthal came back with a bid of $3 million.

Counting Barrett-Jackson's buyer's premium, the Oldsmobile F-88 sold for a Barrett-Jackson Auction record of $3.24 million.

Alan Lewenthal celebrates his winning bid, made in behalf of a new automotive museum that was under construction in Gateway Colorado.

And the action wasn't over. Remember, the F-88 was only one of eight cars on the auction catalog's cover.

A one-of-a-kind 1958 Chevrolet Corvette with a retractable hardtop, created by GM design studio fabricator Francis H. Scott, brought more than $340,000.

Next was a pair of unique Corvettes. Larry Gehrig had been collecting Corvettes for many years and now was selling a unique matched set: an original 1953 model—white with a red interior—and a 50th anniversary convertible, specially built by Chevrolet to match the '53 not only in colors but even in vehicle identification numbers. Each car sold for $297,000.

A 1953 Allard J2X Le Mans factory racer got $399,600. The 1936 Delahaye-inspired and Boyd Coddington–designed street rod *Whatthehaye* brought $540,000. A 1936 Chrysler Airflow custom street rod fetched $550,800. A 1970 Plymouth HEMI Superbird went for $307,000.

Looking back on a sensational Saturday prime-time telecast, even Craig Jackson was astounded. He called the sale of the Oldsmobile F-88 "a moment you may never see again."

Well, at least not until the Barrett-Jackson Auction celebrated its 35th Anniversary in January 2006.

This one-off 1958 Chevrolet Corvette with a retractable hardtop was created by a former GM design studio fabricator, Francis H. Scott, and sold for $340,200 at Barrett-Jackson in 2005.

Corvette collector Larry Gehrig offered a matched set of white Corvettes at Barrett-Jackson in 2005. The one on the top is a unique 50th anniversary edition car that GM had built to match Gehrig's original 1953 Corvette—including the same VIN number (right). The cars sold at Barrett-Jackson for a combined total of nearly $600,000.

Old race cars with good pedigrees have become favorites among modern car collectors. This 1953 Allard J2X Le Mans factory lightweight race car sold at the 2005 Barrett-Jackson Auction for $399,600.

Custom car builder Boyd Coddington was inspired by the 1936 Delahaye when he created *Whatthehaye*, a street rod that sold at Barrett-Jackson for $540,000 in 2005.

Born as a 1936 Chrysler Airflow and reborn as a customized street rod, this cool car went for a hot $550,800 at Barrett-Jackson in 2005.

Prime time Saturday night at Barrett-Jackson 2005 turned out to be a historic feeding frenzy among car collectors. This 1970 Plymouth HEMI Superbird was snapped up for $307,800.

A variety of tents covers acres and acres of collector vehicles at the 2006 Barrett-Jackson Auction in Scottsdale.

CHAPTER 4

Creating the Ultimate Collector Car Event

The 35th Anniversary Barrett-Jackson Collector Car Auction figured to be the biggest yet.

THE FIRST OFFICIAL AUCTION EVENT occurred on Saturday, January 14, with the second annual Drive the Dream Gala, which attracted 800 people to what has become one of the top annual social/charitable events in the Phoenix area. The event, this year featuring jazz guitarist George Benson, raises money for Childhelp USA, which since 1959 has assisted abused and neglected children throughout the United States.

This was just the first of a succession of charity benefits that are part of the Barrett-Jackson Auction each year. During the auction itself, several cars were donated for sale, with $3 million raised for causes such as Childhelp USA, Carroll Shelby Children's Foundation, the Darrell Gwynn Foundation, and the Make-a-Wish Foundation.

Preparations are made for the Drive the Dream Gala, an event that raises money for Childhelp USA.

Sunday, January 15, marked a new part of the Barrett-Jackson Auction lifestyle experience—the first Family Value Day. It can cost as much as $50 per person for admission to the auction grounds for the Saturday night prime-time action. But Craig Jackson wanted to grow the base of not only bidders but of those who might like a glimpse of what all the buzz was about. With admission set at $10 for adults, $7 for students and senior citizens, and with no charge for youths age 12 or younger, he offered the Family Value Day. There was no bidding on any cars, but all the vehicles were on display, and there were about 350 vendors and many food stands.

Jackson said one seed for Family Value Day had come from Corky Coker, former president of the Specialty Equipment Market Association (SEMA), the trade group for automotive aftermarket producers and others involved in the auto industry. Coker, whose family produces tires for vintage vehicles, wanted a way to make sure the next generation learns about cars at an early age and started his "Take a Kid to a Car Show" campaign.

"I didn't know what to expect," Jackson admits. "We guessed maybe three to five thousand people."

As it turned out, lots of people brought their kids to Barrett-Jackson's inaugural Family Value Day. "We had twelve thousand adults and twenty-five thousand people on-site," Craig Jackson reports. "What amazed me was how many 'soccer moms' were there with their kids having a great time, and who would never have come to the auction on another day."

Pete Yanovitch and his father join Darrell Gwynn (center) and Barrett-Jackson's Steve Davis to watch the action as the bidding builds on a car donated to help raise money for Gwynn's foundation that benefits those with spinal cord and other debilitating illnesses and injuries. Gywnn, a champion drag racer, was critically injured in a racing mishap.

This 1978 Chevrolet Corvette convertible was donated for auction to raise money for the Darrell Gwynn Foundation. The car brought $75,000, then was redonated by the new owner and brought another $43,200 on its second trip across the block.

Childhelp USA founders Sara O'Meara (left) and Yvonne Fedderson (right) are joined by actor Rick Schroder and his wife, Andrea, at the Drive the Dream Gala.

George Benson performs at the Drive the Dream Gala that officially kicks off the 35th Anniversary Barrett-Jackson Auction.

Former Indianapolis 500 winner Arie Luyendyk is a regular visitor to the Barrett-Jackson Auction, both at its charity events and as a participant in the auction itself.

With its new Family Value Day program, the Barrett-Jackson
Auction truly has become a family affair.

FOR SEVERAL YEARS, Craig Jackson and the City of Scottsdale, which holds the lease on the WestWorld equestrian and event grounds complex, had battled over infrastructure. Access roads. Parking. Tents. But especially drainage. More precisely, they battled over what Jackson saw as a lack of drainage.

The Valley of the Sun may be one of the driest metropolitan areas in the United States, but when it rains, it doesn't just pour, it puddles—at least it did at WestWorld, and for several years in a row, it rained on the Barrett-Jackson Auction. It's bad enough when spectator parking lots are flooded; it's something else when, as in 2005, collector cars are suddenly up to their rocker panels in standing water.

Barrett-Jackson had survived—in fact, it had thrived—in the face of the Gulf War, despite the invasion of Iraq, even after September 11, and Craig Jackson was not going to let the auction simply drown from lack of drainage.

Despite the auction's impact on the local economy, despite the auction's long history of supporting local charities, despite the auction's roots in the *Fiesta de los Auto Elegantes,* Craig Jackson wasn't getting what he needed from his landlord, so he started looking at options.

The flooded polo field at WestWorld in 2004 was just another event that made Craig Jackson look at other sites for the Barrett-Jackson Auction.

Some figured he might move the auction to Las Vegas. After all, Jackson often compared the change in the collector car business to the way Las Vegas had changed—from a place for gambling, cheap buffets, and even cheaper women to a place where families went on vacation. But Jackson didn't want to move, not to Las Vegas, not even across the Valley to Glendale, the up-and-coming community that had lured the Phoenix Coyotes hockey team and the Arizona Cardinals football team with new, side-by-side stadiums.

Still, Glendale's offer was more than attractive. But Jackson called his legal team and said he wanted one more run at Scottsdale.

"Scottsdale has the resorts. Scottsdale has the culture. It's where I live," Jackson says. "I didn't want to drive to Glendale every day."

Much to Jackson's delight, "the City of Scottsdale stepped up." It agreed to improve the WestWorld infrastructure. It agreed to provide perhaps the world's largest structure—nearly a quarter-mile long, some 100 yards wide, and eight stories tall, spanning nearly 300,000 square feet with seating in front of the auction block for 8,000 people.

Care is taken in unloading vehicles such as this rare Mercedes-Benz 300SL Gullwing.

Continued on page 62

More than 4,800 people registered to bid at the 2006 Barrett-Jackson Auction.

Craig Jackson honors the matriarch of the company, Nellie Jackson, at the Opening Night gala.

On Monday, January 16, registered bidders and auction participants had exclusive access to WestWorld to see the vehicles and to begin using the concierge services provided by the Scottsdale Convention and Visitors Bureau, with on-site reservations for everything from dinner to golf to sightseeing to a day at a spa.

That evening was the annual invitation-only Opening Night Gala, with more than 6,500 people inside the big tent for a special auction preview, food from 20 of the Valley's leading restaurants, 32 open bars, and live entertainment by—how fitting—Mitch Ryder and the Detroit Wheels.

Continued from page 60

Scottsdale also agreed to expand the paved area around the auction and exhibition tents, improve drainage on the polo fields where collector cars are parked on display, and enhance WestWorld access.

For 2006, Barrett-Jackson would have a venue befitting the even bigger show that Craig Jackson was planning— an event that spanned two weekends and featured 34 hours of live television coverage, with more than 1,100 vehicles crossing the block.

The first of those cars arrived at WestWorld on Monday, January 9. Crews from Barrett-Jackson, the City of Scottsdale, and their various suppliers had already been working for more than three months to get the site ready for the vehicles' arrival.been working for more than three months to get the site ready for the vehicles' arrival.

Cars and their paperwork are carefully screened during the check-in process at the 2006 Barrett-Jackson Auction at Scottsdale.

"It's Craig's guest list," says Judi Yates, whose Schneider-Yates & Associates plans major charitable and corporate events. "It's Craig's way of thanking his bidders and letting them enjoy themselves."

The gala was held on Monday night because, for the first time, the 2006 auction spanned six days, beginning on Tuesday, January 17, and running through Sunday, January 22. But the vehicle auction wouldn't be the only show. Each year, Barrett-Jackson also stages a concurrent automobilia auction of such things as dealership signs, hood ornaments, transportation toys, gas pumps, posters, and more. There is also what is known as the Lifestyle Pavilion where vendors offer everything from model cars to jet airplanes, from automotive art to luxury homes, from fashion and furs to, well, fun.

"We have a very diverse product mix," says Mike Laurel, who has managed Barrett-Jackson's vendor program since 2000, when there were just slightly more than 150 vendors at WestWorld. "Some of it is unique, almost humorous, and there can be a very spontaneous appeal. It's a buying atmosphere. Something catches somebody's eye and the conditions are just right.

"I came from an event production background— consumer shows like boat shows, home shows, recreational vehicle shows," Laurel adds. "I expected the majority of booths at Barrett-Jackson would be auto-related, but we've strived to make it more of a lifestyle event. About sixty-five percent of our vendors are nonautomotive.

"Our vendors have good, quality merchandise," he continues. "We attract a good percentage of upscale people, and they enjoy buying things."

Automobilia offered at Barrett-Jackson includes gas station and dealership signs as well as a variety of old gas station pumps.

Not everyone can afford to go home from Barrett-Jackson with a collector car. In fact, some people don't collect cars, but they may collect car posters or other automobilia.

Sure, it's a collector car auction, but cars aren't the only things for sale at Barrett-Jackson. Fur coats and other clothing are popular items available at vendor booths.

Hungry? Barrett-Jackson offers a variety of food, from local Southwestern favorites to salmon shipped down from Alaska.

High-end consumer goods are popular with Barrett-Jackson customers, so the vendor area offers such things as massage chairs, which can provide a relaxing pit stop from walking around the acres and acres of WestWorld.

Signs of the times, even from the old times.

Collectible cars come in lots of sizes.

Right and Opposite:
**Ford's corporate
sponsorship includes a
drifting exhibition area
at Barrett-Jackson, where
various high-performance
Fords burned through
lots of rubber.**

"THERE WERE TWO GUYS, PROBABLY
IN THEIR EARLY TWENTIES WHO HAD
COME FOR THE DRIFTING EXHIBITION,
AND I OVERHEARD ONE OF THEM SAY
TO THE OTHER, 'HEY, I HEAR THERE'S
AN AUCTION A QUARTER-MILE DOWN
THE ROAD IN THAT TENT. MAYBE WE
SHOULD TAKE A LOOK.'"

—STEVE DAVIS

The installation of a larger tent at WestWorld allowed Laurel to add around 50 vendors for 2006, but even then he had to work within space restrictions, especially with the auction attracting two major corporate sponsors. "

For 2006, the Barrett-Jackson Auction's two major corporate sponsors were long-time supporter DaimlerChrysler and newcomer Ford Motor Company, who both had major vehicle displays, with Ford providing such entertaining features as a drifting track where people could experience one of the newest forms of motorsports competition.

Barrett-Jackson executive vice president Steve Davis remembers taking a few minutes away from the auction to walk down to watch a pair of Ford Mustangs sliding around the track, their engines at full song and smoke billowing from their rear tires.

"There were two guys, probably in their early twenties who had come for the drifting exhibition, and I overheard one of them say to the other, 'Hey, I hear there's an auction a quarter-mile down the road in that tent. Maybe we should take a look.'

"Here's a couple of young guys, really digging this thing, really living the lifestyle," Davis says. "That's really indicative of what we've been able to create."

Such creativity included *The Barrett-Jackson Experience*, a slick-paper 102-page magazine published in partnership with Primedia. The magazine was designed to help educate car-collecting newcomers to the various aspects of the hobby. Regular features include car comparisons—why one 1955 Chevrolet Bel Air hardtop sells for $46,600 and a seemingly identical one goes for $221,400; features on cars and car collectors; how-to stories such as "Nine Fun Things to do with a Collector Car Once You Have One"; or simply how to register to be a bidder at next year's auction.

On Wednesday, January 18, the focus of the Barrett-Jackson lifestyle experience was the annual Designer Fashion Show, which is actually two shows. The first features high-end clothing from a major store; for 2006 it was Dillards. The second is more eclectic, this year with fashions from eight local boutiques.

In keeping with the spirit of this lifestyle event, those in attendance were handed champagne for the first show, martinis for the second.

"The word is out," says Judi Yates, who notes that more than 800 people—men and women, she adds—fill the seats for each show.

Family days and fashion shows are fun, and certainly have become part of the Barrett-Jackson Auction experience. But now, at last, it's time for the real show to begin.

Ford brought in a chassis dyno to show just how much power its cars put to the pavement—you could actually drive the quarter-mile.

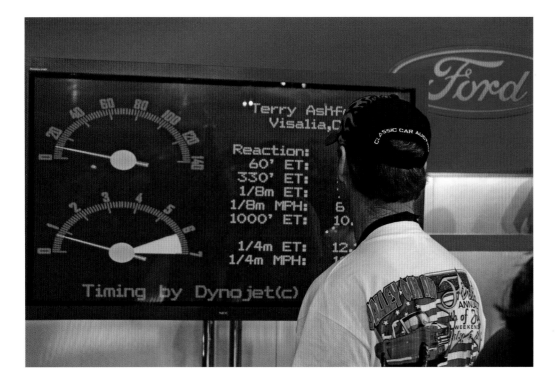

The Chrysler Group and DaimlerChrysler have been a major sponsor of Barrett-Jackson for a decade. Its display includes a variety of vehicles.

A pair of fashion shows spice up the 35th Anniversary Barrett-Jackson Auction. One featured designer wear from Dillards, the other an eclectic collection from eight Scottsdale area boutiques. Even Arie Luyendyk Jr. was pulled from the crowd to participate.

A bright green 1970 AAR Plymouth 'Cuda and other cars draw a crowd to the staging lane, where cars get their final touch ups before rolling onto the auction block.

CHAPTER 5

The 35th Anniversary Barrett-Jackson Collector Car Auction

If you think parking is hard to find at WestWorld during the Barrett-Jackson Collector Car Auction, you should see the congestion on the tarmac at Scottsdale Airport, a City of Scottsdale–owned facility and one of the nation's busiest single-runway airports.

THE AIRPORT IS THE HUB OF SCOTTSDALE Commerce Airpark, home to 2,200 businesses, with national headquarters for more than two dozen companies. It also is home to some 450 aircraft and several outstanding private car collections.

The airport can handle seemingly any sort of private plane or corporate jet, and the end of its 8,249-foot runway is just across the expressway from the entrance to WestWorld and the Barrett-Jackson Auction.

More than 200 Barrett-Jackson bidders arrive in their own airplanes, and the number seems to grow almost exponentially each year.

Craig Jackson likes to tell the story of one collector who flew in for the auction in 2004 and brought six of his friends along in his private jet. In 2005, each of those friends flew his own private jet to Scottsdale, and each brought several other friends along.

FOR 2006, IT APPEARED THAT everyone and all of their friends were at Barrett-Jackson, with 225,000 people in attendance—and that doesn't count the average of 781,000 households (with a high of 1.6 million) viewing the event during the 33 hours of live television

More than 200 of the bidders at the Barrett-Jackson Auction arrive in their own airplanes, which creates quite a parking jam at nearby Scottsdale Airport.

A pair of Mercedes-Benz 350 SLs was carefully unloaded in anticipation of crossing the block at the Barrett-Jackson auction in January 2006.

coverage by SPEED. As a result, the cable outlet enjoyed some of the highest ratings in its 10-year history. In fact, during the Barrett-Jackson Auction time slots on Tuesday and Wednesday nights, SPEED enjoyed the highest ratings in its history for those days and time slots.

"Clearly, the added hours we chose to dedicate to the Barrett-Jackson Auction were well deserved," said Rick Miner, SPEED vice president of programming and production, "and our viewers responded by watching in record numbers."

Particularly impressive were the ratings for men aged 18–34—the demographic so sought after by advertisers. Barrett-Jackson's ratings among that group were up 86 percent over the previous year.

"The Barrett-Jackson brand continues to deliver impressive numbers in multiple formats," added Hunter Nickell, SPEED's executive vice president and general manager. Nickell explained that not only do the live auctions (from Scottsdale and Palm Beach) bring in large audiences, but "the one-hour specials and behind-the-scenes series provide strong programming throughout the year."

Crowds gather to examine the cars in the staging area just outside the big auction tent.

"CLEARLY, THE ADDED HOURS WE CHOSE TO DEDICATE TO THE BARRETT-JACKSON AUCTION WERE WELL DESERVED, AND OUR VIEWERS RESPONDED BY WATCHING IN RECORD NUMBERS."
    –RICK MINER, SPEED VICE PRESIDENT OF PROGRAMMING AND PRODUCTION

In addition to the standard live auction coverage, SPEED and Barrett-Jackson offered "Fantasy Bidding" to television viewers, who could place imaginary "bids" on 33 different cars during the course of the auction. Unlike real bidders, the fantasy bidders didn't have to submit verifiable lines of credit; they are just testing their skills at predicting how much each of these 33 vehicles would bring when it rolled across the auction block. Nearly 24,000 viewers took part in the vicarious experience.

While collector cars are the stars at Barrett-Jackson, they aren't the only items available as several hundred vendors offer everything from Alaskan salmon chowder to gas station memorabilia and from scale-model cars to high-end consumer goods.

IN THE MONTHS LEADING up to the auction, consignors contacted Barrett-Jackson to make known the availability of their vehicles—6,000 of them. Even with the expansion of the auction to six days, there would be space and time to handle only 1,100 of those vehicles.

Consignors weren't the only ones turning out in record numbers. People from all 50 states and 14 foreign countries, 4,852 to be exact, registered to bid on those vehicles.

"Barrett-Jackson is different than any other car sale on the planet because of the number of buyers," explains Keith Martin, publisher of *Sports Car Market*, a magazine that covers the collector car industry.

"At most auctions, there may be a one-to-one or even a two-to-one ratio of buyers to cars," Martin continues. "But at Barrett-Jackson you have four thousand registered bidders chasing one thousand cars. At this auction, you have four buyers for every car. You also have a higher targeted selection of cars—muscle cars, retro rods, modifieds, whatever. All these people are chasing this very specific niche, so the prices become quite high and often are not replicable outside this superheated atmosphere."

Craig Jackson agrees with much of Keith Martin's analysis, though he recalls that Martin once predicted that the auction would never top $25 million in sales, and adds that people come to Barrett-Jackson for both the quality and the quantity of the vehicles offered. He also adds that private sales of collector cars sometimes are transacted for even more money than changes hands at the auction.

When Craig Jackson's father, Russ, and his partner, Tom Barrett, were running the company, the collector car hobby revolved around the classic cars: prewar Duesenbergs and Packards, Hispano-Suizas, and such. American 1950s cars full of chrome and big fins and vehicles such as Gullwing Mercedes became more or less modern classics. Then, in the late 1980s, there was the speculation-driven surge in the prices of exotic European sports cars—Ferraris, Lamborghinis, and such.

Craig Jackson noticed that while speculators were simply interested in cars as investment vehicles, the great cars weren't being turned over as the market ebbed and flowed. They were bought by passionate people building their collections, and only sold when those people were experiencing significant changes in their lives, or after their lives ended when the cars became available as part of an estate.

Another popular car during the bubble period: A 1991 Lamborghini Diablo.

"I grew up watching Tom Barrett selling all of those classics," Craig Jackson says. "There were a lot of people back then from the World War II generation. I saw that the World War II generation, when they became empty nesters and had all this money, they were Tom Barrett's clientele. Then I started doing a little bit of research on the baby-boomer generation, when they would be empty nesters with all their wealth."

Like the World War II generation, Jackson knew that the boomers—people like his late brother, Brian—were passionate about cars and wanted to build collections rather than flip the cars for profit. He also knew that the boomers represented not only a huge group, but one with diverse interests and, with things such as vintage races and vintage road rallies and cruise-in nights in so many communities, they could exercise both their passions and their cars.

Big-finned Detroit iron holds up well in the collector car hobby. Shown here are a 1959 Cadillac Eldorado convertible (right) and the slightly less decoratively finned 1960 model. *Photo courtesy of Nina Russin*

Jackson not only identified his target audience—and an audience that would have many more people and much more money than even the World War II generation—he realized early on that their automotive interests were different. Like his brother, Brian, the baby boomers were into muscle cars and Corvettes and anything even closely related to Carroll Shelby.

Desirable then and now: A 1963 Ferrari SWB.

This newest generation of car collectors also coveted the cars it wanted but couldn't have in high school. "I'm buying what my daddy wouldn't buy me when I was in high school," says collector Allan Jones.

"We're experiencing a generational, monumental shift in the collector car hobby," says Steve Davis. "With television and our live events and our website, Barrett-Jackson reaches millions and millions of people," he says, and more are exposed to cars through the popularity of movies such as *Gone in 60 Seconds*. "As a result, what used to be this really well-kept secret in the small community of car guys has infected other people. We're bringing more and more and more people in every single day. We've created an awareness and the hobby has reacted."

Davis says that in 2004, 2005, and again in 2006, 40 percent of those buying or selling at Scottsdale were newcomers.

The split-window was gone, but the 1964 Chevrolet Corvette coupe has remained a sought-after collector car.

A sad irony, Craig Jackson admits, is the aftermath of the attack on the World Trade Center in 2001. "After 9-11, people realized we may not live forever," Jackson says. "The attitude is, 'I've worked hard my whole life. I've always dreamed about doing this. Now is the time to do it. Tomorrow may never come.' "

"The number of people who have an affection for muscle cars is much larger, and the wave of the sea that we baby boomers represent is a large one," adds Keith Martin. "This swell of wealth and delayed gratification and end-game automotive purchase—'I'm going to have a HEMI before I die'—is sweeping over the collector car market."

Jackson also realized that the *American Graffiti* generation liked more than just muscle cars and even more than 'Vettes and Shelbys. This new generation of car collectors has much more eclectic tastes than did its forefathers. It likes muscle, but it also likes hot rods and customs, and it even still has an appreciation for the classics and for vintage sports cars. And with cable television promoting car customization, Jackson recognized that boomers might even come to see people such as Boyd Coddington and Chip Foose as contemporary coachbuilders, creators of one-off vehicles that would become as collectible as those built many decades ago by the famous French, Italian, British, and American craftsmen.

Custom motorcycle builder Paul Yaffe is among the celebrities taking part in the 2006 Barrett-Jackson Auction.

FOR THE 2006 BARRETT-JACKSON AUCTION, seven cars were selected for the catalog cover, illustrating the change in car collector tastes. After the Oldsmobile F-88 concept car set a Barrett-Jackson record in 2005, it figured that the catalog cover centerpiece was another GM Motorama concept car: the 1954 Pontiac Bonneville Special. Yet another concept, the 1952 Chrysler d'Elegance, also made the cover, as did a pair of Mercedes-Benz 300 SLs—one a 1957 Gullwing coupe, the other a 1963 roadster. Also portrayed were a very special 1967 Chevrolet Corvette convertible, a 1939 Lincoln Zephyr custom by Boyd Coddington, and a 1970 Plymouth HEMI 'Cuda convertible—1 of only 14 from that year and the only one painted in Vitamin C Orange.

Billy Gibbons of ZZ Top is a well-known car collector and Barrett-Jackson celebrity.

The auction also featured the oldest surviving Chevrolet Corvette, the first Ford Shelby GT500 offered for public sale, a group of vehicles with "001" serial numbers—including Baldwin Motion Chevrolet Camaro SS, the 40th Anniversary Shelby GT350SR, and the first Foose-designed 2006 Ford Mustang "Stallion"—Elvis Presley's 1960 Lincoln limousine, and a variety of other cars with celebrity provenance provided by the likes of Sammy Hagar, Bob Seger, Alice Cooper, Billy Gibbons, Bill Goldberg, Randy Johnson, and others.

And there was the largest and perhaps most unusual vehicle ever offered in 35 years of Barrett-Jackson auctions: a General Motors Futurliner, 1 of 12 such buslike vehicles built by GM for its Parade of Progress tour in 1950.

THE AUCTION OPENED ON TUESDAY, a day that surprised Craig Jackson, not because of the numbers being bid, but by the attendance, which was larger than the Thursday attendance from just a couple of years earlier.

With tickets for Tuesday and Wednesday priced at just $20 for adults, "we added a lot of people who were just coming to get the experience of Barrett-Jackson,"

Above: **Michael Anthony, who plays bass for Van Halen and also co-owns bonspeed, offers a signed guitar with the sale of the bonspeed Pontiac Sunfire concept car.**

Van Halen front man Sammy Hagar not only offered his Red Rocker car at the Barrett-Jackson Auction, but the high bidder also got Hagar's guitar and a case of Cabo Wabo tequila.

Craig Jackson says. "We wanted to open the experience to people from whatever walk of life and regardless of their income level. My intention has been to grow the event to have something for everybody."

For Tuesday bidders, there were a couple hundred cars for auction. Claiming top price for the day was a 1967 Plymouth Belvedere GTX hardtop that had undergone not just a restoration, but a HEMI engine transplant as well. It fetched $118,800.

If Tuesday pleased Craig Jackson, Wednesday had a surprise awaiting Steve Davis, because a 1964 Amphicar, a strange vehicle that was part car, part boat, sold for an astounding $124,200.

If anyone on the grounds at WestWorld has a handle on how much vehicles should sell for, it is Davis. But he admitted he had no anticipation that the quirky car would go for anywhere close to six figures, let alone draw the highest bid of the entire day. And as recently as the 2003 Scottsdale auction, $124,200 would have put the Amphicar in the top 20 on the final sales list.

One of the most stunning bids of the 2006 Barrett-Jackson Auction came early in the week when this immaculately restored 1964 Amphicar went for $124,200.

"We're attracting a very eclectic, very individualist collector whose reference is based on values today, not twenty years ago. Our customers compete to buy the best example of whatever car, and this was an unusual vehicle that a lot of people have never been exposed to.

> "WE WANTED TO OPEN THE EXPERIENCE
> TO PEOPLE FROM WHATEVER WALK
> OF LIFE AND REGARDLESS OF THEIR
> INCOME LEVEL. MY INTENTION HAS
> BEEN TO GROW THE EVENT TO HAVE
> SOMETHING FOR EVERYBODY."
> —CRAIG JACKSON

This 1967 Chevrolet Corvette convertible sold for $216,000.

"We have people here with a lot of disposable income and we have a very competitive environment.

"Much like the Futurliner or the F-88, this was a very unusual vehicle, very impactful visually, and it brings bragging rights. When you get home, it's certainly the only one on the block."

As expected, action escalated on Thursday, when three cars shared high-dollar-of-the-day honors as a 1966 Chevrolet Chevelle SS 396 hardtop, a 1962 Chevrolet Corvette FI (fuel-injected) convertible, and a 1958 Porsche 356A cabriolet each drew $135,000.

Also going for $216,000 on Friday of the 2006 Barrett-Jackson Auction was this 1937 Cord 812 Phaeton convertible.

Even with seating for some 8,000 people, things are crowded under the big top.

The $200,000 plateau was achieved five times on auction Friday. A muscle car—1969 Z/28 Camaro coupe—led the day at $221,400, though a 1967 Corvette 427 convertible, a 1969 Dodge Super Bee hardtop, a 1969 Chevrolet Chevelle Copo (Central Office Production Order, a method dealers could use to order cars with excessive horsepower) hardtop, and—let's hear it for the classics!—a 1937 Cord 812 Phaeton convertible all drew $216,000.

THE PRELIMINARIES WERE FUN, then came Saturday—the biggest crowd, on the grounds and on television, packing the tent or sitting in front of TVs to take part in Saturday night showtime when the stars of the 2006 Barrett-Jackson Auction would parade across the auction block. This isn't just prime time. This is showtime!

Prime-time Saturday night at Barrett-Jackson lived up to its reputation as this 1970 Plymouth HEMI Roadrunner coupe sold for $702,000.

In its March 1968 issue, *Hot Rod* magazine called the 1968 Ford Mustang 428 Cobra Jet fastback "the fastest pure stock in history." The car went quickly at Barrett-Jackson in 2006, for $513,000.

Hours before prime time, a 1968 Dodge Dart, a HEMI-powered factory lightweight engineered for drag racing, took bidding above $300,000 as it fetched $324,000. Later, just as prime-time coverage was beginning, a 1970 Plymouth HEMI 'Cuda hardtop topped the $400,000 plateau at $486,000, and the car right after it—a 1968 Ford Mustang 428 Cobra Jet fastback—drew $513,000!

The first of the catalog cover cars—the pair of Mercedes 300 SLs—brought $324,000 (for the roadster) and $372,600 (for the Gullwing coupe).

The next car was a 1970 Chevrolet Chevelle LS6 convertible that had been driven by Ray Allen to victory at just about every conceivable drag race entered in 1970 and was

This 1963 Mercedes-Benz 300 SL convertible offered at Barrett-Jackson in 2006 was part of the final year's production of this model.

Craig Jackson and Ray Allen enjoy the bidding on Allen's 1970 Chevrolet Chevelle LS6 convertible, a car Allen drag raced, winning—among other things—the U.S. Nationals. Allen did a restoration of the car and offered it at Barrett-Jackson, where it won again—to the tune of $1.242 million!

The Shelby Cobra 427 cost $6,400 new in 1966, but it brought $594,000 at Barrett-Jackson 40 years later.

Boyd Coddington has gained superstar status among car collectors for his hot rod and custom cars.

Top right: **A Boyd Coddington–created 1939 Lincoln Zephyr Custom** *Lead Zephyr*, **propelled by a 500-horsepower Ford V-8 engine, traded hands for $345,600.**

The Baldwin Motion Camaro rekindled the famed Baldwin Motion Camaros of the muscle car era, but has all-new mechanicals. The first of this very limited production run sold for $486,000 at Barrett-Jackson in 2006.

Top bid on this 1963 Dodge Polara custom, built by Boyd Coddington (driving) on the *American Hot Rod* television program, drew a top bid of a half million dollars. Part of the proceeds went from Coddington's foundation, which benefits the Make-A-Wish Foundation under Barrett-Jackson's charity car donation program.

recently restored. Add racing history to muscle car mania and the crowd is on its feet as bidding hits $1.242 million.

Another cover car—the #001 Baldwin Motion Camaro—goes for $468,000. A 1966 Shelby Cobra brings $594,000. Another cover car—the Coddington-designed Lincoln Zephyr custom—draws $345,600.

On the auction block at Barrett-Jackson are the rights to the first 2007 Shelby GT500. The winning bidder also won the right to specify color and factory options. (above) Edsel Ford (left) and Carroll Shelby celebrate the sale of the first 2007 Shelby GT500. The car went for $600,000, with proceeds benefiting the Carroll Shelby Children's Foundation.

A 1963 Dodge Polara custom—again by Coddington, with help from 16-year-old leukemia patient Max Cohen—got a stunning $540,000, and since this car was part of the Barrett-Jackson charity program, the money all went to the Make-A-Wish Foundation and the Coddington Foundation.

A 1956 Mercedes Gullwing garnered $621,000, followed by a Foose-designed 1969 Chevrolet Camaro custom ($259,200), the Foose-designed 2006 Mustang Stallion ($167,400), a 40th anniversary edition 1965 Shelby Mustang GT350SR ($307,800), and a 1967 Chevrolet Corvette convertible built for the Corvette factory manager ($216,000).

The stage thus was set for the Bonneville Special, and the anticipation was that a Barrett-Jackson all-time-record bid was about to be seen. On hand were Richard Earl, grandson of Harley Earl—the GM design boss who created not just the Bonneville Special but the entire genre of concept cars—as well as Homer LeGassey, a former GM designer who had helped design and build the car when he was working in Earl's studio.

The Stallion is a 2006 Ford Mustang massaged by Chip Foose and Unique Performance and is the first of a series to be produced. Its new owner paid $167,400 at Barrett-Jackson.

Almost immediately, the bidding surged to $2.6 million, then 2.7, but then it slowed and it appeared the car might not outpace the Olds F-88 and all its drama a year earlier. At $2.8 million Craig Jackson took the microphone and interviewed LeGassey, who talked about how Earl saw the Bonneville as a launching pad to push Pontiac into the youth market and perhaps toward becoming GM's performance division long before "We Built Excitement" would become the marque's motto.

Like the Olds F-88, the Bonneville was largely based on the Corvette, but it featured Pontiac styling cues and a bubble-top roof. At the 1954 Motorama, the Pontiac was a star, eclipsing the Olds. But at Barrett-Jackson, the Olds won the bidding war; the Pontiac sold for $3.024 million, including buyer's premium.

Homer LaGassey and wife Yolanda were on hand to talk about the 1954 GM Motorama concept car, the Oldsmobile F-88, which sold for a record $3.024 million in 2005. In 1954, the bubble-roofed, rocket-tailed Bonneville sent a signal that Pontiac would become GM's high-performance/excitement division.

If Harley Earl had a rival in the 1950s, it was Virgil Exner at Chrysler. Exner's work included the d'Elegance, which was unveiled in 1952. Two years later, Chrysler placed a new 354-cubic-inch HEMI engine under the car's hood. This d'Elegance sold for $1.188 million.

It was a remarkable price—second best in 35 years of Barrett-Jackson auctions—but nonetheless it was a disappointing figure to most people, and it was almost as if someone had sucked the air out from under the big Barrett-Jackson tent.

Next up was another cover car, the 1952 Chrysler d'Elegance. If Harley Earl had a rival in design in the 1950s, it was Virgil Exner at Chrysler, and this was one of Exner's finest one-of-a-kind vehicles. Might this be the surprise car of the auction? When the hammer fell, the d'Elegance was sold for $1.188 million. Again, some seemed disappointed, even though the dollar amount ranked it among perhaps the top half-dozen in the history of Barrett-Jackson's Scottsdale auctions.

But just as everyone was wondering what was happening—had the bubble indeed burst?—the auction took a spectacularly dramatic turn.

It's rare when a vehicle at Barrett-Jackson doesn't actually cross the auction block. Take, for example, the 1950 GM Futurliner Parade of Progress tour bus, which was simply too large to fit on the stage. GM built a dozen of these vehicles for its historic tour, which showed futuristic technologies to Americans as the display buses toured the country.

As a consigner, Steve Davis offered his cars at No Reserve. As executive vice president of Barrett-Jackson, he pushed to make every car available without a hidden minimum price structure that might keep it from actually being sold at auction.

It was time for Lot No. 1307, the GM Futurliner Parade of Progress tour bus. Working as a commentator for SPEED, Keith Martin mentioned that the vehicle's owner had said he hoped the vehicle would sell for at least $600,000. He needn't have worried. Six hundred thousand was the second bid after the Futurliner opened at a half million dollars.

Almost immediately, it was 950, then a million, 1.1, 1.125, 1.4, 1.5, 1.6, 1.7, 1.8, 1.9—that's right, bids were being bumped by $100,000 over and over and over again—until 1.95.

Then it was two million dollars! Then 2.2, 2.4, 2.5, 2.6, 2.8, 2.9, three million dollars!

Needless to say, the tent was rocking.

Then it took off to 3.2, 3.475, 3.5, 3.6, 3.675, 3.9, and finally four million dollars! Or $4,320,000 with buyer's premium.

HEMI 'Cudas are all the rage. This convertible—1 of only 14 built for 1970, and then built as part of the Chrysler executive lease program—drew $2.160 million at Barrett-Jackson in 2006.

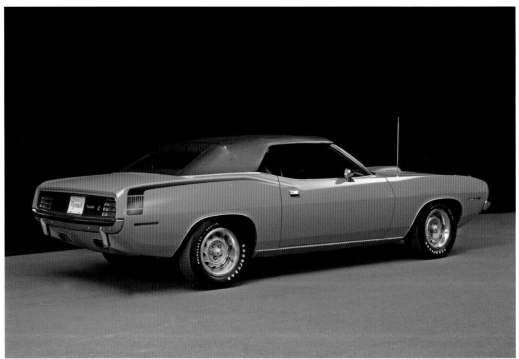

But the show wasn't done yet.

Next up was another cover car, the 1970 Plymouth HEMI 'Cuda's convertible. Of only 14 '70 HEMI 'Cuda convertibles built, this was the only one painted High Impact Vitamin C Orange. Not only was the bidding spirited, but it didn't stop until it reached $2.160 million.

Car collector Dave Ressler is known for wearing—and selling—jackets that match his cars. At Barrett-Jackson 2006, Ressler purchased this 1953 Chevrolet Corvette, serial number 003, making it the oldest original Corvette. The car sold for $1.08 million.

A few weeks after the auction, Craig Jackson tried to put the phenomenon in some sort of meaningful car collector perspective: "They made only 725 Duesenbergs and only 708 HEMI 'Cudas," he said, "and there are more people who want the 'Cudas."

But the auction still was not done. Corvette No. 003 fetched $1.08 million. Elvis' limo got $556,200. A '1972 'Cuda brought $702,000. The six-figure bidding frenzy continued into the night.

Elvis Presley was on active duty in Germany with the U.S. Army when he ordered this 1960 Lincoln limo, which was customized for "The King" turned private by Hess and Eisenhardt and had only 33,000 original miles on its odometer when it sold at Barrett-Jackson for $556,200 in 2006.

Sunday, the final day of the auction, seemed almost anticlimactic, but also delightfully eclectic. A 1941 Willys Americar coupe went for $120,960, a 1912 Kissel Semi Racer brought $149,995, a 1931 Auburn convertible got $172,800, a 1968 Shelby GT500 fetched $194,400—but the day's biggest sale was $270,000 for a 1938 Packard limo built for the William Wrigley family, now powered by the V-10 engine from a Dodge Viper.

This 1931 Auburn cabriolet showed that there's still a lot of interest in classics as it drew $172,800 on the final day of the 2006 Barrett-Jackson Auction.

In celebration of the 35th anniversary of Barrett-Jackson, car collector Dave Ressler presented Craig and Nellie Jackson with a 35th anniversary Chevrolet Corvette. The car was part of a special run of the American sports car, which had its 35th anniversary in 1988.

Starting on Tuesday with a 1964 Vespa motor scooter that brought $2,160 and ending on Sunday with a 1967 Camaro RS/SS coupe that went for $36,720, the 2006 Barrett-Jackson Auction had posted record sales of more than $100 million.

But even after selling more than 1,100 vehicles for more than $100 million, Craig Jackson is a long way from where he wants to be.

This 1953 Chevrolet Corvette convertible is the oldest original Corvette in existence. It brought a winning bid in 2006 of $1,080,000.

The Top 35 Cars from the 35th Year

The following are the 35 top-selling cars from the 35th Anniversary event.

1950 General Motors Futurliner Parade of Progress tour bus

To celebrate America's postwar optimism and potential, General Motors staged the Parade of Progress, a national tour to showcase scientific developments. Displays were carried in a dozen of these tour bus/rolling display stages. Of those that survive, only three have been fully restored, including this one that features air conditioning for the elevated driver's compartment. The selling price for this Futurliner was $4,320,000.

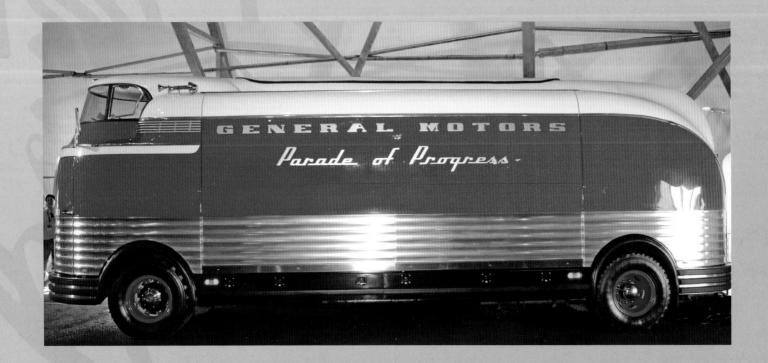

1954 Pontiac Bonneville Special Motorama concept car

To showcase its new production cars and to hint at what the automotive future might hold, General Motors staged its Motorama auto show tour from 1950 to 1961. The stars of the shows were exotic concept cars created to pave the way for new designs and technologies. The Bonneville Special was created after GM design chief Harley Earl returned from watching speed runs on the Bonneville Salt Flats. The car, which shared underpinnings with the Chevrolet Corvette, featured jet-like styling cues, including the bubble canopy roof. This green car (a bronze-colored model toured the East Coast) sold at Barrett-Jackson in 2006 for $3,024,000.

1970 Plymouth HEMI 'Cuda two-door convertible

Nothing seems to rev up a baby boomer's motor like the word "HEMI." Only 14 HEMI 'Cuda convertibles were built for the 1970 model year, and this is the only one that came in High Impact Vitamin C orange paint. It is equipped with the A32 Super Performance axle package with Sure-Grip 4:10 gears and the B51 power brake package, as well as power steering. The car was originally built for a Chrysler Corp. executive and sold at Barrett-Jackson's 35th Anniversary Event for $2,160,000.

1970 Chevrolet Chevelle LS6 convertible

The odometer on this car showed 61 miles as it rolled onto the block at Barrett-Jackson in January 2006. Ray Allen drag raced the car in 1970 and won seemingly every significant event, including the National Hot Rod Association's U.S. Nationals. Allen had recently supervised this historic muscle car's restoration, and his presence and the car's provenance were meaningful to bidders, who ran the price to $1,242,000.

1952 Chrysler d'Elegance two-door hardtop

If GM's design chief Harley Earl had a cross-town rival, it was Chrysler's Virgil Exner. Exner designed a series of marvelous production and concept cars, among them the 1952 d'Elegance—a car that would influence many future designs (in fact, the Karmann Ghia is a miniature model of this design). The 1952 d'Elegance, which sold at Barrett-Jackson for $1.188 million was upgraded by Chrysler in 1954 with a larger 354-cubic-inch HEMI engine, new Torque-Flight transmission, and a 12-volt electrical system. The company also converted the brakes from temperamental discs to drums.

1953 Chevrolet Corvette convertible

With serial number "003," this is the oldest original Chevrolet Corvette in existence, and its odometer showed little more than 300 miles since a full restoration in 1990. This historic car won numerous awards— Bloomington Gold, Corvette Hall of Fame, Duntov Award—and brought a winning bid of $1,080,000.

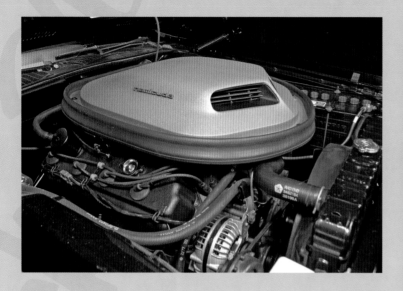

1970 Plymouth HEMI 'Cuda hardtop

The Chrysler Registry documents that this was number 128 of 284 1970 Plymouth HEMI 'Cudas built with four-speed transmissions. This one is a rare "triple-black" version and came with its original engine and gearbox rebuilt as part of the vehicle's extensive restoration. With full documentation and certification, this black beauty went for $702,000.

2007 Shelby GT500 fastback

With both Carroll Shelby and Edsel Ford on hand, bidding on this first of the 2007 Shelby GT500s ran to $600,000, with proceeds from the car—which was donated by Ford Motor Company—going to the Carroll Shelby Children's Foundation. The winning bidder won the rights to the first new Shelby GT500 made available to the public, with the bidder getting to select the color and options on this most powerful Mustang ever built by the Ford factory.

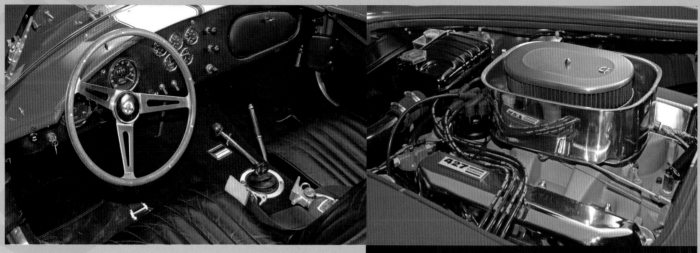

1966 Shelby Cobra roadster

This 1966 Shelby Cobra is set up for vintage racing. Power comes from a stroked, 460-cubic-inch Holman-Moody "side-oiler" V-8 engine verified to pump out more than 500 horsepower. At Barrett-Jackson's 35th Anniversary Event, this Cobra struck for $594,000. A percentage of this sale was donated to the Carroll Shelby Children's Foundation.

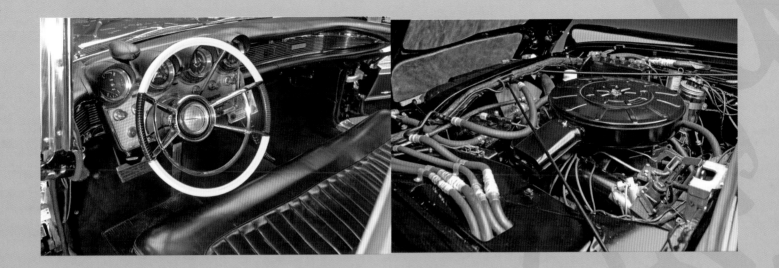

1960 Elvis Presley's Lincoln limousine

Elvis Presley ordered this car while serving in the U.S. Army in Germany in summer 1959. After five years of service to Elvis, the car was sold and had been owned nearly 40 years by the same person until it was offered at Barrett-Jackson, where it sold for $556,200.

1956 Mercedes-Benz 300 SL Gullwing coupe

This car went to Barrett-Jackson just two months after a frame-off restoration. The car had been owned by only two people, both from California, including 38 years by the owner who sold it at the 35th Anniversary Event for $540,000.

1963 Dodge Polara Custom two-door

This customized Dodge was built by Boyd Coddington on the *American Hot Rod* television series, with design and fabrication help from Max Cohen, a 16-year-old leukemia patient, whose greatest wish was to build such a hot rod. This one, complete with a 572-cubic-inch HEMI crate engine and Gabe Lopez interior, was donated with proceeds from its sale—for half a million dollars top bid—going to the Boyd Coddington Foundation, which benefits the Make-A-Wish Foundation.

1968 Ford Mustang 428 Cobra Jet fastback

Considered the fastest of all stock Ford Mustangs, and declared by *Hot Rod Magazine* "the fastest pure stock car in the history of man," the Cobra Jets were built to beat the HEMIs—and they could. This restored car's engine pumps out more than 550 horsepower. It also pumped up bidding with the hammer finally falling at $513,000, including buyer's premium.

1970 Chevrolet Chevelle LS6 convertible

The two-owner muscle car had only 44,000 miles on its clock and had not been shown in public since 1975. It is the only SS 456 LS6 convertible known to exist in this color combination. The restoration retained 100 percent of original parts and date codes, enhancing the car's value at Barrett-Jackson to $513,000.

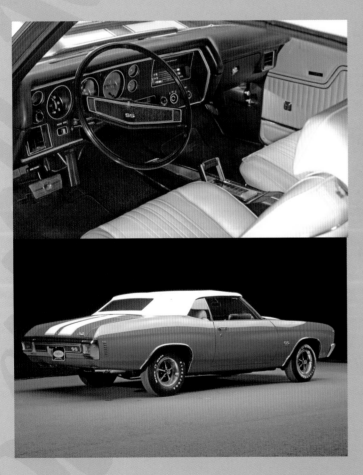

1970 Plymouth HEMI 'Cuda two-door hardtop

This Ivy Green muscle car had been driven less than 100 miles since its complete restoration. Of the 284 HEMI 'Cudas built in 1970 with four-speed transmissions, this is one of only 170 known to exist. This car brought $486,000 at Barrett-Jackson in 2006.

1969 Chevrolet Camaro SS Baldwin Motion coupe

In the heyday of muscle cars, the Baldwin Motion Camaro was one major dealership's way to soup up an already outstanding vehicle. Principals involved in the original Baldwin Motion have reunited to produce a limited run of SuperCoupes powered by a 540-cubic-inch Merlin/Motion big-block engine, five-speed Tremec gearbox, 14-inch Baer Claw Extreme brakes, and more, all mounted on a backbone-style chassis. The first of these modern monsters was offered at Barrett-Jackson in 2006 and went for $486,000.

1969 Chevrolet Camaro ZL1 coupe

Dick "Mr. Chevrolet" Harrell raced this car in 1970. To homologate the car for racing, Chevy had to build at least 50 of these COPO creations, and all of them were ordered by and sold through Fred Gibb's dealership. COPO stood for Central Office Production Order, and the COPO 9560 package included an aluminum ZL1 engine, a cold-air hood, heavy-duty cooling, a transistor ignition, a special rear axle, F70x14 tires, front power disc brakes, and a new Turbo 400 automatic transmission. This car, No. 9 of the 50, sold at the 35th Anniversary Event in Scottsdale for $486,000.

1967 Shelby GT500 fastback

This car had been driven less than 400 miles since its full restoration. With its original 428 engine, four-speed transmission, and Posi-Traction rear end, this car has both matching numbers and Carroll Shelby's personal autograph, all of which fetched $451,000 at the Barrett-Jackson 35th Anniversary Event.

1968 Shelby GT500 KR fastback

This Mustang still wears its original paint and shows its original interior, as well as such things as original tires, belts, hoses, even spark plugs. The car spent a full year at the Carroll Shelby Museum in Las Vegas, and has Shelby's autograph on the inside of its trunk lid. Considered a true time capsule, this GT500 sold at Barrett-Jackson's 35th Anniversary Event for a price of $432,000, including buyer's premium.

1959 Mercedes-Benz 300 SL two-door roadster

There's something magical about the 300 SL Mercedes. Take this one, an "older" restoration that still sold for $432,000 at Barrett-Jackson in 2006.

1967 Ford GT40 Mk V

GT40s were race cars that won at Le Mans four years in a row, but this one, chassis P1096, has never been to the track. In fact, it still rides on its original tires, which have traveled less than 5,000 miles. This historic car sold at Barrett-Jackson's 35th Anniversary Event for $396,000.

1953 Ford Vega Roadster "Gardner Special"

Ford Motor Company, which was celebrating its 50th anniversary, and Motor Trend magazine jointly sponsored a design contest, and this was the winner. Designed by Vince Gardner, who was part of Gordon Buehrig's team that created the Cord 810, the car has an aluminum body and had been hidden away for more than 40 years until it was offered at Barrett-Jackson, where it brought $385,000 (including buyer's premium).

1957 Chrysler Imperial convertible

Howard Hughes bought this car new in 1957 and used it for a few years before putting it in storage. Brian Jackson bought the car in 1976 and subsequently sold it. It came out of storage again at the 35th Anniversary Barrett-Jackson Event, where it drew a price of $378,000, including buyer's premium.

1967 Chevrolet Corvette 427/435 convertible

Selling for $378,000 at the 2006 Barrett-Jackson Event, this matching-numbers and restored Corvette features factory-installed side pipe exhaust and has been twice featured in Corvette Enthusiast magazine.

1957 Mercedes-Benz 300 SL Gullwing coupe

This coupe and a 1963 300 SL convertible were offered at the 2006 Barrett-Jackson Scottsdale Event by the same owner. This Gullwing was unrestored, though a one-owner car with 55,849 miles on its odometer. It sold for $372,600.

1939 Lincoln Zephyr Custom *Lead Zephyr*

Boyd Coddington ended a hiatus from custom vehicle building, and this stunning custom was his comeback car. This unique Lincoln Zephyr rides on air suspension and one-off wheels. Propulsion comes from a 430-cubic-inch Ford V-8 that pumps out 500 horsepower. Bodywork was done by Marcel and Sons; the interior was done by Gabe's Custom Upholstery in tan leather and wool carpet. Price at Barrett-Jackson 2006 was $345,600.

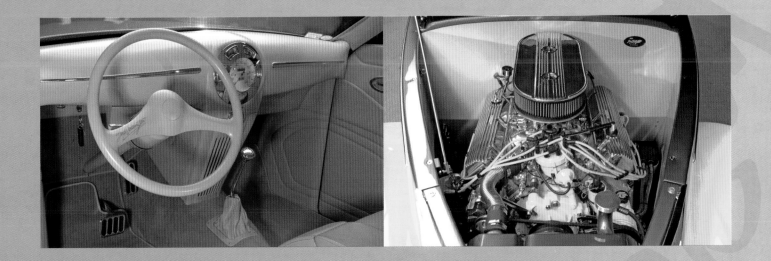

1965 Shelby GT350 fastback

A 1,300-hour restoration transformed this classic Mustang into a car that brought a price of $335,880 at the 2006 Barrett-Jackson Event.

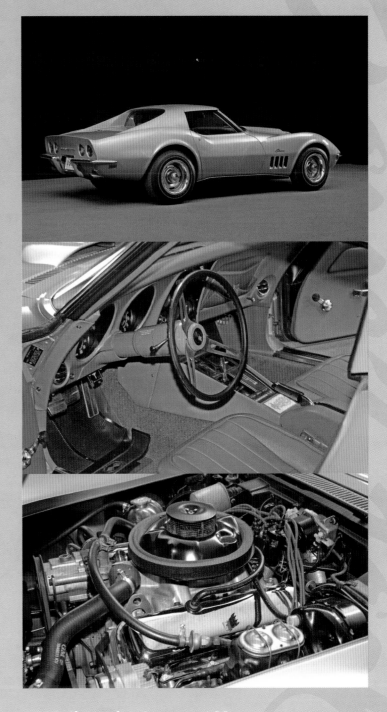

1969 Chevrolet Corvette L88 coupe

The lowest-mileage 1969 L88 Corvette known to exist and one of only 116 L88s built by the factory, this 430-horsepower American sports car spent much of its life on display at the Gilmore Classic Car Museum in Michigan. It sold at Barrett-Jackson for $334,000.

1963 Mercedes-Benz 300 SL convertible

This is the convertible offered alongside the 1957 Gull-wing coupe (at right). This convertible was produced in 1963, the last year of production for the famed 300 SL line. It showed 34,483 miles on the odometer, but only 50 since the original owner had Mercedes-Benz rebuild the inline-six-cylinder engine. The convertible brought $324,000

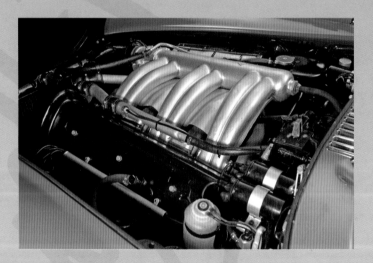

1968 Dodge HEMI Dart two-door hardtop

This factory lightweight car drew a price of $324,000 at the 2006 Barrett-Jackson Event. The drivetrain features a 426-cubic-inch HEMI V-8 and an automatic transmission.

1965 Shelby GT350SR Ford custom fastback

Carroll Shelby and Unique Performance celebrated the 40th anniversary of the SCCA B/Production champion 1965 GT350R Shelby Mustang by producing a limited series of GT350SR Mustangs, with the first one offered for auction at Barrett-Jackson Scottsdale in 2006. Power comes from a 427-cubic-inch small-block Shelby Engine rated at 585 horsepower. Other features include independent front and adjustable rear suspension, Tremac five-speed transmission, Baer disc brakes, and custom blue interior. No. 001 got $307,800.

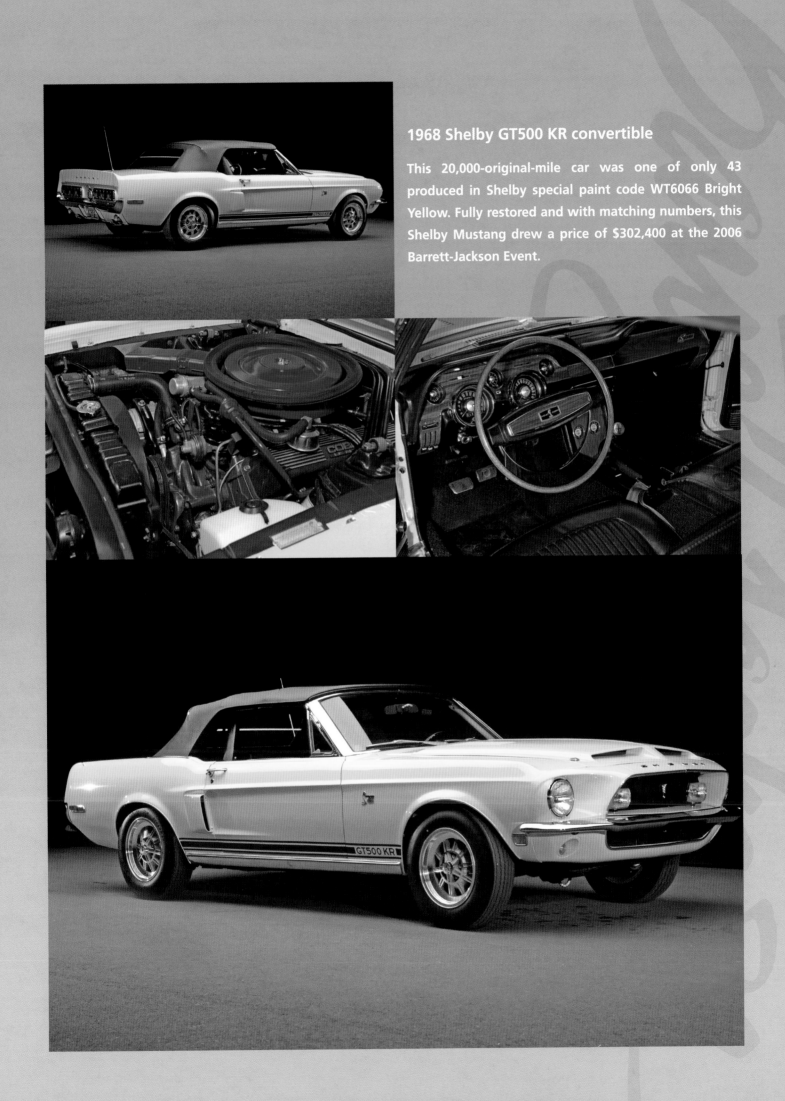

1968 Shelby GT500 KR convertible

This 20,000-original-mile car was one of only 43 produced in Shelby special paint code WT6066 Bright Yellow. Fully restored and with matching numbers, this Shelby Mustang drew a price of $302,400 at the 2006 Barrett-Jackson Event.

1957 Chevrolet Corvette ZL1 convertible

When Bill Elliott retired from full-time NASCAR racing, racing fabricator Kent Waters had some time on his hands, so he widened the rear quarter panels on this Corvette by two inches, put that body on a tube frame chassis, and added a new rear end, Tremec five-speed transmission, and a 650-horsepower 454-cubic-inch aluminum ZL1 big-block engine. A custom exhaust, Wildwood brakes, and many other custom features are included, among them a black-and-red Ostrich skin interior. The car made its debut at Barrett-Jackson in 2006 and sold for $291,600.

1938 Packard custom limousine

This stretched Packard limousine originally was built for the William Wrigley (chewing gum) family, but has been updated with such goodies as a Viper V-10 engine, six-speed transmission, power steering, and disc brakes. It brought a price of $270,000 on Sunday of the 35th Anniversary Barrett-Jackson Event.

1962 Ford Galaxie Factory Lightweight

Known as "Thunderbolts," there were eleven of these cars built in 1962 for the "factory experimental" drag racing category -- A/FX. Of those 11 Fords, only four are known to have survived. This one brought $270,000 at Barrett-Jackson. Thunderbolts were built to be light and fast. That meant they were equipped with a fiberglass hood, fenders and trunk, had no sound deadening materials, special aluminum bumpers and radiator, and didn't come with radios or even heaters. But they did get 406 cubic inch high-performance V8 engines.

Of course, you can't have an auction without auctioneers, and it takes a large crew to handle all the cars and bidders at Barrett-Jackson.

"HOW DO YOU DEAL WITH THIS?" the grad students asked.

They wanted to know how the temporary auction facilities were built—and then dismantled—at WestWorld. How all the logistics were handled. And they especially wanted to know how all of those temporary employees were trained.

"They were blown away," Craig Jackson remembers.

For one thing, Jackson says, there are job descriptions for every job, and with those job descriptions there are "answer sheets."

"The first person you run into when you come to the auction is the parking lot attendants," Jackson says. "They have to know where to send you. Then there's the person at the gate. They have to know where the office is or the answer to whatever question you may have. Whatever it is, you have to get the right answer no matter who you ask."

Jackson has made a practice of attending major events, automotive and motorsports and nonautomotive events, and of examining their temporary-employee training handbooks.

"We've put a good core of people in the full-time positions," Jackson says.

In addition to their regular departmental duties, the full-time staff spends a lot of time in the run-up to the auction training the temporary staff, many of whom come

Ellen "Nellie" Jackson's official title is executive director of Barrett-Jackson. At 87, Nellie still comes to the office every day to supervise daily operations.

Under Carroll Shelby's hat and behind the shades is Steve Davis, senior executive vice president of the Barrett-Jackson Auction Company. His duties include scheduling the order in which cars will be offered for bidding.

back year after year after year and thus may not need much training, just a quick refresher and update.

"The best compliment I can get is to hear people say that our auction is the best-run event, that everybody is treated well, that there's attention to detail, and that problems are taken care of immediately," Jackson says.

That, by the way, was the conclusion of the Harvard students' study.

"That," says Jackson, "I find gratifying."

Gary Bennett, shown with his wife, Audra, is the senior automotive specialist for Barrett-Jackson. Like Steve Davis, he was a long-time Barrett-Jackson customer who brought years of automotive expertise to the auction company.

Patrick van den Bossche, shown with his wife, Denise, is chief operation officer of Barrett-Jackson.

Tony Riddick (left) is a graphic designer and Enrique Chavez is a site crew manager and has one of the longest tenures of all Barrett-Jackson employees

Right: Hank Bried's title is security director. He's been part of the Barrett-Jackson team for a decade.

Shelly Drake is executive assistant to Craig Jackson.

Right: **Casey McDonald** is the Barrett-Jackson Auction site/operations director.

John Cook (front seat) is a consignment liaison. Left to right in the back seat are Mandy Dye, consignment liaison, and Jill Smith, consignment manager. The consignment staff work with the people who bring vehicles to the auction for sale.

Left: **Jamie Breitbach is** the project manager at Barrett-Jackson.

Right: **Janie Davis is a** consignment liaison and the wife of Steve Davis, executive vice president.

Holly Moeller (front seat) is the bidder manager for the Barrett-Jackson Auction and Katherine Matterson is a bidder representative, who helps register the thousands of bidders for the event.

Betty Oser is a bidder representative and has been a valued staff member and friend for many years.

Information technology manager Jason Rose (left), marketing specialist Jen Schmitt (center), and marketing director Deb Klein-Stokes.

Ginger Wilber is the photography and media manager.

Bill Hamilton is the systems engineer, in charge of various communications systems at the Barrett-Jackson Auction.

Michael LaPier is Barrett-Jackson's hardware engineer.

Mike Laurel is the vendor manager, lining up the hundreds of booths where auction attendees can buy everything from model cars to paintings, clothing and so much more that is part of the Barrett-Jackson automotive lifestyle.

Jason Rose is a technician assistant and is so lucky to be able to maintain and drive amazing vehicles on a daily basis.

Luke Barosky is the guest services manager and Danica Levy is the guest services representative. During the auction, they train more than 50 individuals to answer guests questions on the phone or at the auction site.

Deborah Fifer (left) is the Barrett-Jackson controller and Denise Danner is the human resources representative.

Susan Valdez (left) and Denise Taylor are Barrett-Jackson staff accountants.

Kristen Quint is the SPEED television liaison and thus works closely with Barrett-Jackson's senior executive vice president Steve Davis, who determines the order in which the vehicles will cross the auction block.

Dave Deuble is the car check-in manager at the Barrett-Jackson Auction.

For many years Judi Yates has tackled the huge role of hospitality coordinator, with lots of help from Deb Schneider (right).

Mary Beth Anderson publishes the Barrett-Jackson Auction catalog.

Rory Brinkman directs the Automobilia portion of the Barrett-Jackson Auction. In addition to the collector cars that are up for bidding, items such as vintage gas station pumps, automotive dealership signs, pedal cars and much more are offered for auction each morning.

Several of the auctioneers at Barrett-Jackson have a lot in common. Many are from Texas, and many of those from Texas are named Assiter. That includes lead auctioneer Tom "Spanky" Assiter.

Attractive bidders assistant Amy Sparks quickly became a star of SPEED's telecasts, but she, too, became an Assiter when she married lead auctioneer Tom "Spanky" Assiter.

Mark Gellman has been calling the Barrett-Jackson Auction since 1978 even though he's neither from Texas (he's from California) nor is his last name Assiter.

Top left: **Tim Assiter is a seller's ambassador.**

Top right: **Kenton Merrihew has been part of the Barrett-Jackson Auction team since 1997 and works as a seller's ambassador.**

Middle right: **Craig Jackson joins auctioneer Jimmy Landis on the auction podium.**

Bottom: **Bandy Assiter is a bidder assistant.**

Bart Haythrone is the auction clerk, sort of an official scorer in charge of keeping track of who bid how much on what and who gets the car when the hammer falls.

John Nichols (left) and Tom "Spanky" Assiter are auctioneers. Nichols, from Virginia, has been part of the Barrett-Jackson Auction team since 2000.

Mitch Armitage, from Oklahoma, is a bidder assistant, working the auction floor to make sure his bidder's bids are relayed to the stage.

Tom Johnson (yes, he's from Texas) is a bidder assistant who made his Barrett-Jackson debut at the 35th Anniversary event.

Craig Davis (yes, he's also from Texas) is a bidder assistant who has worked the Barrett-Jackson Auction since 2004.

James Grant (a Texan) is a bidder assistant who makes sure his bidder has time to consider raising the bid.

Whitey Mason (from Oklahoma) is a bidder assistant and appears to be the calm eye in the center of storm that sometimes takes place on the bidding floor.

Roger Spencer (from Pennsylvania) is another bidder assistant, and he'll kick up a storm to make sure his bidder's offers reach the stage.

Can't wait for the next auction? Barrett-Jackson has a showroom in a former Rolls-Royce dealership building in Scottsale, Arizona, where a variety of collector cars available for immediate sale.

CHAPTER 7

The Future

On the eve of the 35th Anniversary Barrett-Jackson Auction at Scottsdale, Motor Trend *magazine published its annual Power List of the 50 most powerful people on the planet in the automobile industry.*

THE LIST INCLUDED THE HEADS OF the major car companies, and people such as megadealer and racing team owner Roger Penske, BMW's controversial design director Chris Bangle, Formula One racing czar Bernie Ecclestone, and the living legend, Carroll Shelby. And for 2006, that list included Craig Jackson.

Under Craig Jackson's leadership, the Barrett-Jackson Auction Company grew from a mom-and-pop shop that was selling—not offering, but actually selling—maybe 400 cars a year for around $15 million, to one that in 2006 sold some 1,500 vehicles for nearly $140 million, including the Scottsdale and Palm Beach events.

Through live television coverage of the auctions at Scottsdale and Palm Beach, through taped programming in the months leading up to the auctions, and through its website and its own magazine—as well as coverage in national newspapers and major magazines (and not just automotive magazines, but business magazines as well)—Barrett-Jackson has exposed car collecting and an automotive enthusiast lifestyle to millions of people, many of whom increasingly have come to accept Barrett-Jackson as not merely a trendsetting auto auction company, but as a vacation destination like Las Vegas or Walt Disney World, and even as a brand in its own right.

Yet in Craig Jackson's mind, he's just getting started.

"I STARTED HEADING TOWARD A GOAL TEN YEARS AGO," Craig Jackson says, explaining that he saw a parallel developing between the World War II and baby-boomer generations in their passion for collecting classic cars. He recognized that while their definition of "collector" cars may have changed, their passion was the same.

Jackson is convinced that "we're not just riding a bubble like we did in the late eighties."

"This isn't Japanese money or guys buying cars who just want to flip them the very next day. Back in the late eighties, a lot of people who didn't even care about cars got into it strictly as an 'investment.' I don't get a sense of that nowadays. Guys and gals now have a passion. They're building collections. It's the same thing that happened with the classics.

"They're taking part of their disposable income and building their collections, and they're doing it with a small percentage of their net worth. This is what they want to do with part of their money.

"Even if cars go down some in price, I don't see them wanting to have a fire sale. They're having fun."

ONE OBVIOUS DIFFERENCE between the collectors of the classics and the collectors of muscle cars, resto mods, customs, and 1970s stock car–based drag racers is what they consider to be collectible cars.

Once upon a time, except for people who might want to collect one Model T for every year it's been in production or as many Chevrolet Corvairs as would fit into a barn or building, "collector car" meant pre–World War II classics—tall, long, and large, and usually with very squared corners, vehicles such as Model J Duesenbergs, dozen-cylindered Cadillacs, 1930s Mercedes, and those coachbuilt cars with all of those amazing French curves—or significant sports cars, such as the Gullwing Mercedes-Benz 300 SL and the early cars from Enzo Ferrari's stable of the Prancing Horse.

The 1956 Mercedes-Benz 300SL Gullwing coupe sold at Barrett-Jackson's Scottsdale auction in 1995.

Turn the clock back just a dozen years and look at the half-dozen cars that brought the most money at the Barrett-Jackson Auction in 1995:
• 1952 Ferrari 225 S two-door Spyder ($312,375)
• 1936 Cadillac V-16 convertible coupe ($299,250)
• 1956 Mercedes-Benz 300SL Gullwing ($200,550)
• 1935 Auburn 851 Speedster ($181,125)
• 1931 Packard 845 Rollston Victoria convertible ($162,750)
• 1953 Chrysler Ghia coupe ($162,750)

(Note: Four Ferraris—a 1971 365 conversion, a pair of 1973 365 GTB/4 Daytona coupes, and a 1967 330 GTS convertible—rounded out the top 10, and the rest of the top 20 was dominated by cars produced in the 1930s.)

Though the prices were substantially higher, the theme was the same in 1996:
• 1930 Bentley Speed Six ($1,100,000)
• 1933 Duesenberg Rollston ($850,000)
• 1961 Ferrari 250 GT SWB California Spider ($800,000)
• 1929 Bentley 6.5-liter Barker ($750,000)
• 1929 Duesenberg J Murphy roadster ($650,000)
• 1967 Ferrari 275 GTB/4 Berlinetta ($252,000)

The theme was the same in 1997:
• 1929 Duesenberg Le Baron convertible sedan ($750,000)
• 1934 Packard 12 Le Baron coupe ($500,000)
• 1973 Ferrari 365 GTB/4 ($450,000)

This 1932 Stutz DV32 Victoria sold for $399,000 at Barrett-Jackson in 1997.

- 1932 Stutz DV 32 convertible coupe ($399,000)
- 1964 Rolls-Royce Silver Cloud III Muliner Parkward ($375,000)
- 1959 BMW 507 Roadster ($367,500)

And again in 1998:
- 1973 Ferrari 365 GTS/4 Daytona Spyder ($349,650)
- 1973 Ferrari 365 GTS/4 Daytona Spyder ($322,875)
- 1931 Cadillac 452 A Phaeton ($262,500)
- 1967 Ferrari 275 GTB/4 ($244,650)
- 1948 Tucker 1002 sedan ($241,500)
- 1966 Ferrari 275 GTB/2 coupe ($215,250)

But by 1999, the leader board was changing:
- 1973 Ferrari 365 GTS/4 ($304,500)
- 1966 Shelby Cobra 427 Dragon Snake ($299,250)
- 1967 Ferrari 275 GTB/4 Speciale coupe ($256,200)
- 1966 Shelby Cobra Roadster ($238,875)
- 1959 BMW 507 Roadster ($215,000)
- 1959 Rolls-Royce Silver Cloud I Coupe de Ville ($200,000)

This 1966 Ferrari 275 GTB coupe rolled across the block at Scottsdale in 1994.

(Note: Nothing older than 1966 made the cut; only two of the top 20—and they were numbers 17 and 18—were built before World War II. An apparent generational shift was occurring, with renewed interest in cars with an affiliation to Carroll Shelby—the man for whom Craig Jackson had named his daughter, his first-born.)

The mix was similar in 2000:
- 1966 Shelby Cobra 427 Roadster ($381,600)
- 1931 Packard 840 Waterhouse Victoria ($344,500)
- 1948 Tucker Sedan ($333,900)
- 1957 BMW 507 Roadster ($288,850)
- 1927 Bugatti Type 43 Grand Sport ($265,000)
- 1963 Mercedes Benz 300 SL Roadster ($238,500)

(Note: The rest of the top 20 was just as fascinating, including a 1934 Bugatti Type 57, a couple of 1934 Packards, a 1998 Dodge Viper GT2, a four-year-old Lamborghini Diablo, and the 1959 Chevrolet Corvette Italia by Scaglietti.)

The watershed may have been 2001, the first year with Steve Davis in charge of consignments and the actual auction docket that determines which vehicles will be part of the Saturday night prime-time telecast on SPEED:

- 1931 Duesenberg J Murphy Convertible Coupe ($575,000)
- 1952 Chrysler d'Elegance Ghia Coupe ($334,800)
- 1966 Shelby Cobra 427 Roadster ($297,000)
- 1966 Shelby Cobra 427 Roadster ($245,160)
- 1957 Mercedes-Benz 300 SL Roadster ($226,800)
- 1998 Shelby Series I ($217,080)

(Note: Foreshadowing the coming sea change in the collector car marketplace was the fact that among the top 20 in 2001 was a 1934 Ford Deluxe three-window hot rod designed by Boyd Coddington.)

Top left: **Collectors love Bugattis. This Type 43 Grand Prix racer was built in 1927 and brought $265,000 at the 2000 Barrett-Jackson Auction.**

Top Right: **Only 51 of these Tucker Torpedos were built, and they have remained extremely popular among car collectors. This one sold for $333,900 at the Barrett-Jackson Auction in Scottsdale in 2000.**

The 1934 Ford three-window coupe is a collectible in its own right, but its value can increase dramatically when it is turned into a hot rod.

The 2002 North American International Auto Show at Detroit featured Ford's new GT concept car. A couple of weeks later, the 2002 Barrett-Jackson Auction at Scottsdale featured an original Ford GT40:

- 1966 Ford GT40 Mk. I Coupe ($405,000)
- 1966 Ferrari 275 GTB/2 Berlinetta ($264,600)
- 2000 Ferrari 360 Modena Spider ($259,200)
- 1958 Mercedes-Benz 300 SL Roadster ($234,900)
- 1967 Shelby Cobra 427 Roadster ($266,800)
- 1967 Chevrolet Corvette L-89 Roadster ($221,400)

This 1967 Ford GT40 was used to attract showroom traffic to Midwestern Ford dealerships. The car was at Barrett-Jackson in 2003, still wearing its original Goodyear gold-line tires. It sold for $347,760.

The 2003 Barrett-Jackson Auction was more of the same:
- 1967 Ford GT40 Mk. I ($347,760)
- 1967 Ford GT40 Mk. III Coupe ($318,600)
- 1966 Shelby Cobra 427 S/C Roadster ($253,800)
- 1967 Shelby GT500 E Fastback ($253,800)
- 1965 Ferrari 275 GTS Roadster ($183,600)
- 1932 Auburn Cabriolet Coupe ($180,360)

(Note: More foreshadowing: Also in the top 20 were a 1933 Ford Ardun hot rod, the 1970 Plymouth 'Cuda from the *Nash Bridges* television show, and a 1970 Ford Mustang Boss 429 SuperBoss "Lawman" drag car.)

MORE THAN A DECADE EARLIER, Craig Jackson had made a mental note about a car that sold at Barrett-Jackson. The car was a hot rod. But not just any hot rod. This car, the *Alumatub*, had been designed by Boyd Coddington and was powered not by a flathead Ford or even a Chevy small block, but by a turbocharged, four-cylinder engine. To make it even more unusual, it was built not from steel, like so many hot rods, but from aluminum.

Where others saw an interesting one-off vehicle, Jackson saw what he thought might be the first drop in a change in the mainstream of car collecting.

Hot rods had been a staple of car culture ever since the days of the Model T. Even the Chevrolet brothers first gained fame for hopping up the Model T engine. In 1932, Henry Ford put the flathead Ford V-8 into production, and hot rodding was really off to the races. Just two years later, Ford received a handwritten letter praising his fast machines: "I have drove [*sic*] Fords exclusively when I could get away with one. For sustained speed and freedom from trouble, the Ford has got every other car skinned." The letter was signed by Clyde Champion Barrow, of the infamous duo of Bonnie and Clyde.

From the dry lakes of southern California's desert to the city streets on the East Coast, hot rods were symbols of rebellious youth and later of fond nostalgia. Why, in 1997, even the prestigious Pebble Beach Concours d'Elegance, the bastion of classic car culture, added a class so hot rods could be displayed on the hallowed 18th fairway on the shores of the Pacific Ocean.

But just as hot rods were being accepted, they were also changing. No longer content to simply soup up a flathead Ford and set it into an old if refurbished roadster, hot rodders were turning to modern coachbuilders for custom bodywork, and they weren't restricting their palettes to antique chassis. Even conservative Toyota commissioned a Lexus-powered hot rod from Rod Millen, and car collector Eric Zausner had Steve Moal build the Torpedo, a hot rod inspired by old Alfa and Ferrari race cars and powered by a 12-cylinder Ferrari engine.

The *Alumatub* was the third of Boyd Coddington's "Aluma" series that also included a coupe and a pickup truck. Inspired by a 1929 Ford, this aluminum-bodied car is powered by an aluminum block Chevrolet V-8 engine.

Craig Jackson had been right—the genre was changing.

Then, at the Barrett-Jackson Auction in Scottsdale in 2002, the 1954 Plymouth "Sniper" sold for $162,000. The Sniper was designed by Chip Foose and built by Troy Trepanier and his Rad Rides by Troy. What had gone into production nearly 50 years earlier as a basic, beyond-plain-Jane Plymouth Belvedere convertible emerged as a radical rod powered by the V-10 engine from a Dodge Viper.

So now we had traditional hot rods and street rods and customs, and in 2004 something new crossed the block at Barrett-Jackson, something called a "Resto-Mod." "Resto" was short for "restoration" and "mod" was short for "modified." What that meant was a new class of collector cars, cars that look pretty much stock, but underneath that refurbished and only slightly modified sheet metal beats a modern, high-performance powertrain and suspension.

This 1929 Ford hot rod pickup is *Loaded*. That's the hot rod's name, but it also describes the load of trophies and magazine covers it hauled away before selling at the 2006 Barrett-Jackson Auction.

"It's a blend of modern technology with older bodies," says Jackson. "It's a trend you're going to see for quite a while."

By 2004, rods and racers were the rage at Barrett-Jackson:
- 1938 Lincoln Zephyr V12 coupe Street Rod ($432,000)
- 1955 Mercedes-Benz 300 SL Gullwing ($394,200)
- 1955 Mercedes-Benz 300 SL Gullwing ($367,200)
- 1951 Allard J2-Cadillac Le Mans Racecar ($324,000)
- 1937 Cord 812 Supercharged Phaeton ($324,000)
- 1957 Mercedes-Benz 300 SC Roadster ($324,000)

(Note: Also in the top 20 were several Corvettes specially tweaked by tuner Reeves Callaway, and interest in muscle cars pushed a 1970 Plymouth HEMI 'Cuda to more than $200,000 while a resto mod 1955 Chevrolet Bel Air coupe went for more than a quarter million dollars.)

The Gullwing Mercedes, nicknamed because of the way its doors, which incorporate most of the vehicle's roof, open and close, ranks not only as a modern but an all-time collector car classic.

Then, of course, came 2005 and the bidding battle for the Motorama Oldsmobile:
- 1954 Oldsmobile F-88 Concept Car ($3,240,000)
- 1938 Chrysler Airflow Custom 2-door street rod ($550,800)
- 1936 Delahaye "Whatthehaye" street rod ($540,000)
- 1953 Allard J2X Le Mans Factory Lightweight Racer ($399,600)
- 1963 Shelby Cobra 289 Roadster ($388,800)
- 1957 Chevrolet Bel Air "Chezoom" custom ($372,600)

(Note: Five of the remaining top 20 cars were muscle cars, and just to show that classics are still appreciated, a 1932 Auburn Boat-Tail Speedster and 1932 Lincoln KB four-door sport touring also were among the top 20.)

By 2006, the top end of the collector car market had skewed to concepts and muscle cars, and prices had skewed as well:
- 1950 GM Futurliner Parade of Progress Bus ($4,320,000)
- 1954 Pontiac Bonneville Special Concept Car ($3,024,000)
- 1970 Plymouth HEMI 'Cuda 2-door convertible ($2,160,000)
- 1970 Chevrolet Chevelle LS6 convertible ($1,242,000)
- 1952 Chrysler d'Elegance 2-door hardtop Concept ($1,188,000)
- 1953 Chevrolet Corvette # 003 convertible ($1,080,000)

The *Whatthehaye* was another Boyd Codding-ton original. Inspired by a 1936 Delahaye, this street rod draws its power from the V-10 engine usually used in the Dodge Viper.

(Note: Four of the top 20 cars were Plymouth HEMI 'Cudas; three others were cars with Shelby's name on them.)

"Barrett-Jackson has been an incubator," says Steve Davis. "We've created more aware-ness for concept cars and for resto mods and muscle cars and high-end street rods. We've created awareness among qualified people in the arena. Take all of those and combine them and that's the magic you see.

"The F-88 was the turning point. We'd sold cars like that before. In fact, we'd sold the F-88. But there's a difference in the amount of awareness and interest we had cre-ated. You have millions of people interested. At the end of the day, we've changed the landscape of the collector car hobby as we've known it.

"Look at the art world," Davis continues. "Someone pays $23.5 million for a painting and people don't blink an eye, because we've been programmed to understand the value of Rembrandt and other pioneers in the art world.

"It's the same with the top end of collector cars, and especially the concept cars," Davis contends. "These cars represent much more than a utilitarian device to get people from point A to point B. They are American treasures. They represent amazing works of art, American art.

"Value is what someone's willing to pay. What is it? What does it represent? What does it represent to the individual?"

"What our customers have is a lot of money," Craig Jackson acknowledges. He also knows that with that much money, "They can buy cars from a multitude of places.

"But," he says, "a lot of these guys don't have time to go through *Hemmings* [the thick, monthly magazine composed almost exclusively of collector car and car parts classified advertising] or to get on eBay [the auction website with a selection of collectible cars on its eBay Motors site]."

Even if they had time to read and to surf, "they don't have the time to fly around the country to look at those cars," Jackson adds.

Woodys are highly desired by collectors. This 1940 Ford Woody Wagon brought $189,000 at Scottsdale in 2006.

"They choose to buy their cars here. They trust us. They like the experience of buying a car here [and to buy the best of those cars on live national television], and they like the idea of the charity auctions as well.

"They know they can come here with the passion they have and they get to buy the car of their dreams."

CRAIG JACKSON ALSO HAS A DREAM. Well, actually more than one.

He wants to make Barrett-Jackson not only a destination for an auction under a huge tent each January, but a year-round and permanent destination for car enthusiasts. He also wants to leave a legacy on the collector car… well, traditionalists still call it a hobby, but in Jackson's eyes, it's become a full-fledged, multimillion—no, he'll tell you, actually it's a multibillion—dollar industry involving restorers and collectors, SEMA suppliers and magazine publishers, and auction consignors and bidders, with television covering it all and turning Boyd Coddington and Chip Foose and even "Ferrari hat guy" into celebrities.

And, of course, there's Carroll Shelby, who once battled with Enzo Ferrari and who now holds the same position of honor that *il Commendatore* used to possess in the hearts and minds of auto enthusiasts.

Craig Jackson is well on his way to moving Barrett-Jackson from a collector car auction to a lifestyle experience and a widely recognized brand name.

"Money can buy you so many tangible items," he says, "but what matters is the experience you have. I've gone to almost all of the biggest events—to NASCAR, to the

World Series, the Kentucky Derby, the Super Bowl. But there you're a spectator. At Barrett-Jackson you can jump up on the stage and be a player. You can buy the car of your dreams and have the experience on live television."

Jackson wants to expand not only the audience for car collecting, but the number of collectors, and sees television and Barrett-Jackson's website and magazine as ways to help educate the newcomers.

"There are millions of baby boomers looking for something to do other than to go play golf," he says.

But just like golf, there's a price to joining the fraternity—buying golf clubs, taking lessons, joining a country club, flying off to Scotland to play golf with your buddies. "Add it all up," notes Steve Davis, "and did it cost you fifteen-hundred dollars for the clubs or two-hundred-fifty thousand for the experience?

"But it really doesn't matter," he adds. "It's a lifestyle. It's an experience. And that's what we are packaging and selling at Barrett-Jackson."

And, says Craig Jackson, it doesn't have to cost you seven figures to have a collector car that you can enjoy. "You have cruises and road rallies and vintage racing. You don't have to have a car with matching numbers to go to a cruise-in and have a good time."

Jackson beams when he talks about a woman he met at the Barrett-Jackson Auction in Palm Beach, a woman who sought him out to tell him about the pleasure he's brought to her husband, who watched the auctions on television and finally started coming in person and how now it's an activity that they do as a couple.

"It's so gratifying to hear that and it makes all the hard work worth it," Jackson says.

Another spin on the Ford Model A. These 1930 customs are a matching pair that toured the show circuit as a *2 Alarm Fire*. The coupe (left) sold for $97,200 and the roadster (right) sold for $100,400.

"When I planted this seed," he adds, "I knew it could happen."

JACKSON HAS A COUPLE MORE SEEDS HE'S PLANTING. One is a permanent home for Barrett-Jackson adjacent to the WestWorld complex in Scottsdale.

Several years ago, he bought acreage adjacent to WestWorld. His plans include not just a new corporate headquarters and Barrett-Jackson showroom, but a permanent building to house the auction—and other events—as well as a sort of country club for car collectors, a place where they can store, restore, maintain, and drive their collector cars when they're in town.

"I have great customers," Jackson says. "I love hanging out with them. And while this is a business, it's also my personal hobby." Jackson has more than 20 collector cars in his own collection, and those include two vintage race cars—a Trans-Am series AMC Javelin and an AAR 'Cuda. He also likes to do vintage sports car rallies. And with an eye on the car's future collectability, he recently bought a Ford GT—and not just as an investment to be stored in the garage; he regularly drives it to the Barrett-Jackson Auction offices.

"I want our new facility to be a destination for any car enthusiast. It will have a restaurant and a gift shop and a restoration facility, and 'industrial condos' where people can work on their cars, and storage for collector cars in a club atmosphere.

"It's a place where I want to hang out."

Jackson hopes to have the new facilities built this decade. In fact, he feels an urgency to complete the project soon. "I'm forty-six," he says, quietly adding, "My brother died when he was forty-nine."

BUT WHETHER HE LIVES TO BE 49 OR 99, Craig Jackson has a mission that he feels is even more important than building Barrett-Jackson's new home: He wants to leave the collector car hobby in a better state than in which he found it.

"My goal is to have a quantifiable way of rating collector cars."

For example, he says, take four 1965 Ford Mustangs. One is stock original, perhaps not in perfect condition, but original all the way through. Another car has been fully restored, but by someone who used parts made in China and had the car painted by a neighborhood collision repair shop. Yet another car has been restored by a well-respected restoration shop using all NOS (new old stock) parts. And the fourth Mustang has undergone a full resto mod treatment.

"How do you rate all four of those?" Jackson asks. "And when someone reads that a 1965 Mustang sold for $15,000 over here and the 'same' car sells at Barrett-Jackson for $45,000, their perception is that this one was a good value and there are idiots over here.

"But that one was painted at an undependable local shop and has bad components and this one's NOS.

"And you can have 12 Mustangs and they're all from 1965 and they're all original but from different build dates and they're all going to be different. A Monday car is going to be different from a Friday car and they're both different than a car built in midweek. It's hard to get an even balance. There are so many anomalies, especially with General Motors cars."

What Jackson wants to do is establish criteria that will be accepted as the collector car industry standard.

"Coins have price guides that take all these variables into account. Stamps have it. Diamonds have it," he says.

"It's a hard thing to do, but that's what we're really going to try to focus on in our new facility. I want it to be a test/incubation center, to set up a criteria like an under-writers laboratory for aftermarket parts and vehicle restorations."

Jackson also wants to address the safety factor of collector cars.

"You have guys building street rods with stuff from overseas and they're taking them out on the streets and you're going to get a few guys killed using faulty parts, and the government will crack down on the entire hobby. We need to do something to stop that before they do. We have to educate people about what to look for, and that includes the quality of parts and safety.

"I want to make that. If I leave a legacy, that's part of the legacy I want to leave, that I tried to clean this up, I tried to add some credibility to it, a code of ethics of what you should expect when you buy a collector car, what you should look for, how you should be treated, and safety and everything else should go into it. You need to make it fair and safe."

BIBLIOGRAPHY

Periodicals

"Collectors Frenzy in Arizona," by Larry Edsall, *AutoWeek*, January 2, 2006

"Rear-View Mirror: 1954 Oldsmobile F-88," by Michael Lamm, *Consumer Guide*, August 8, 2005

"The Last Great American Carnival," by Steve Cole Smith, *AutoWeek*, March 21, 2005

"When Worlds Collide," by Mark Vaughn, *AutoWeek*, May 13, 2002

Television

Barrett-Jackson Collector Car Auction, live coverage, SPEED Channel, January 2006

Life on the Block, Lingner Group Productions, SPEED Channel, 2005

INDEX